For all the little princesses of the world, who find magic in every stroke of color. May the joy of coloring these pages transport them to realms of dream and imagination. May each brushstroke be a reminder of how special they are and capable of creating their own fairy tale. With love and enchantment, this book is dedicated to you

Pamela Oliveira

2024

This Book Belongs to:

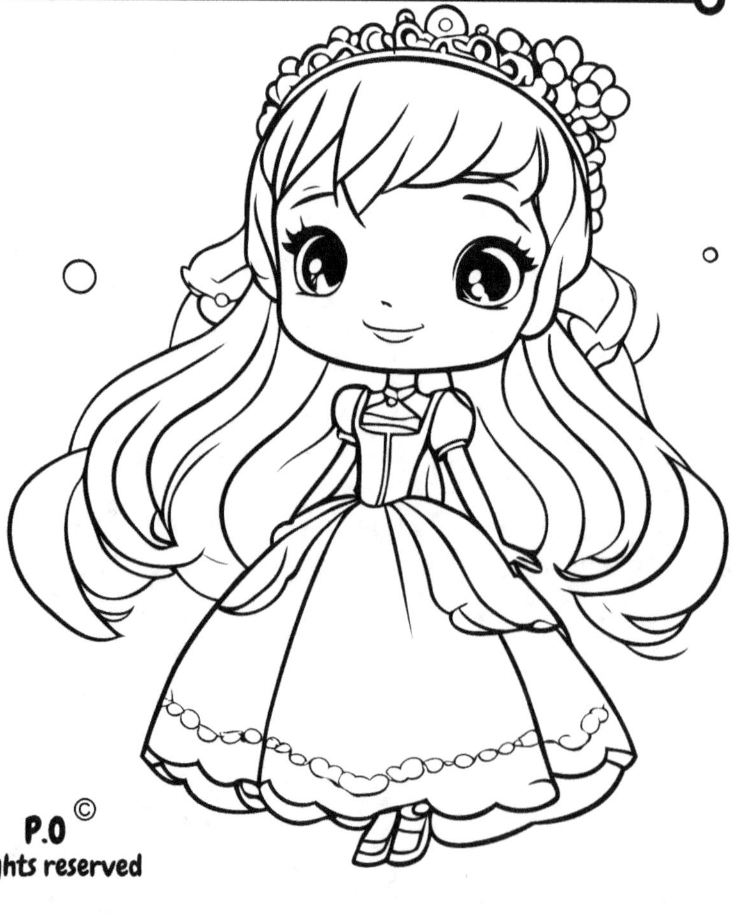

_____

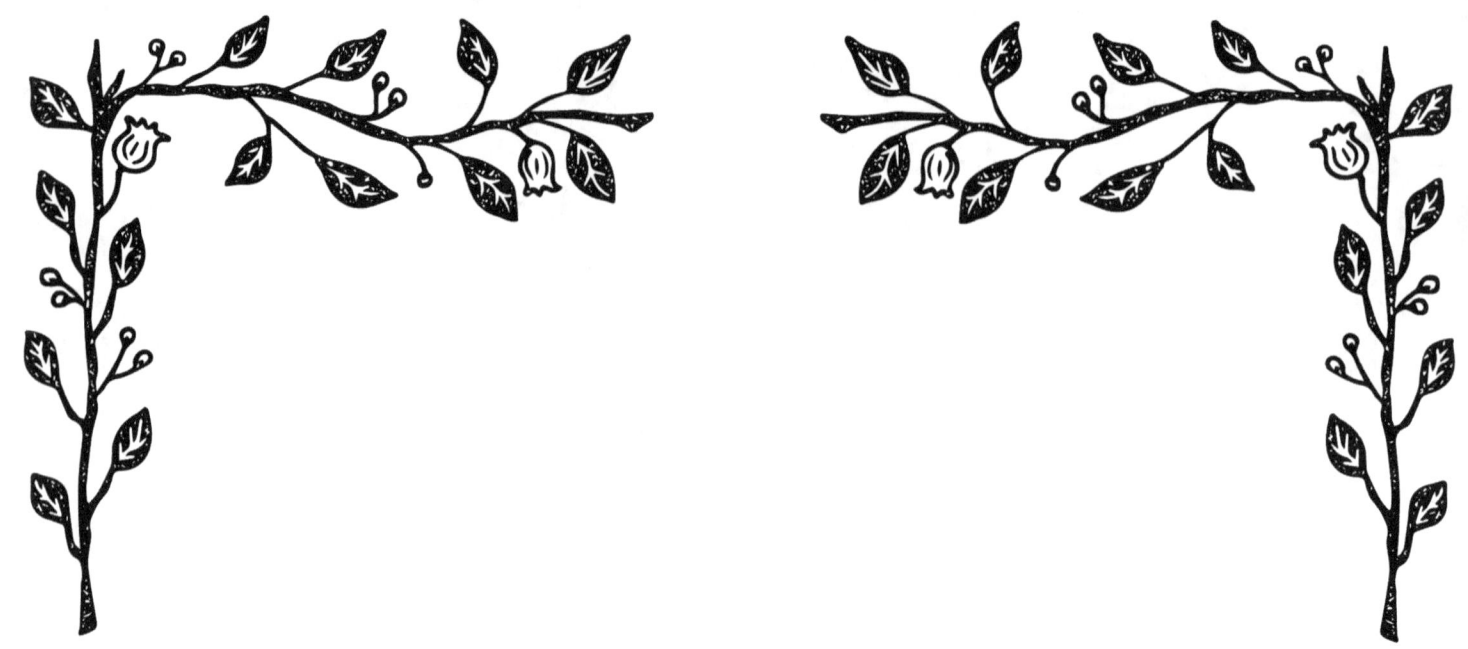

P.O ©
all rights reserved

ALL RIGHTS RESERVED©
2024

No part of this publication may be reproduced, distributed, or transmitted in any form or by any means, including photocopying, recording, or other electronic or mechanical methods, without the prior written permission of the publisher, except for brief quotations incorporated in critical reviews and other specific noncommercial uses. Any unauthorized replica of this work is prohibited.

P.O.P.©
pamela oliveira publications

Test Color Page

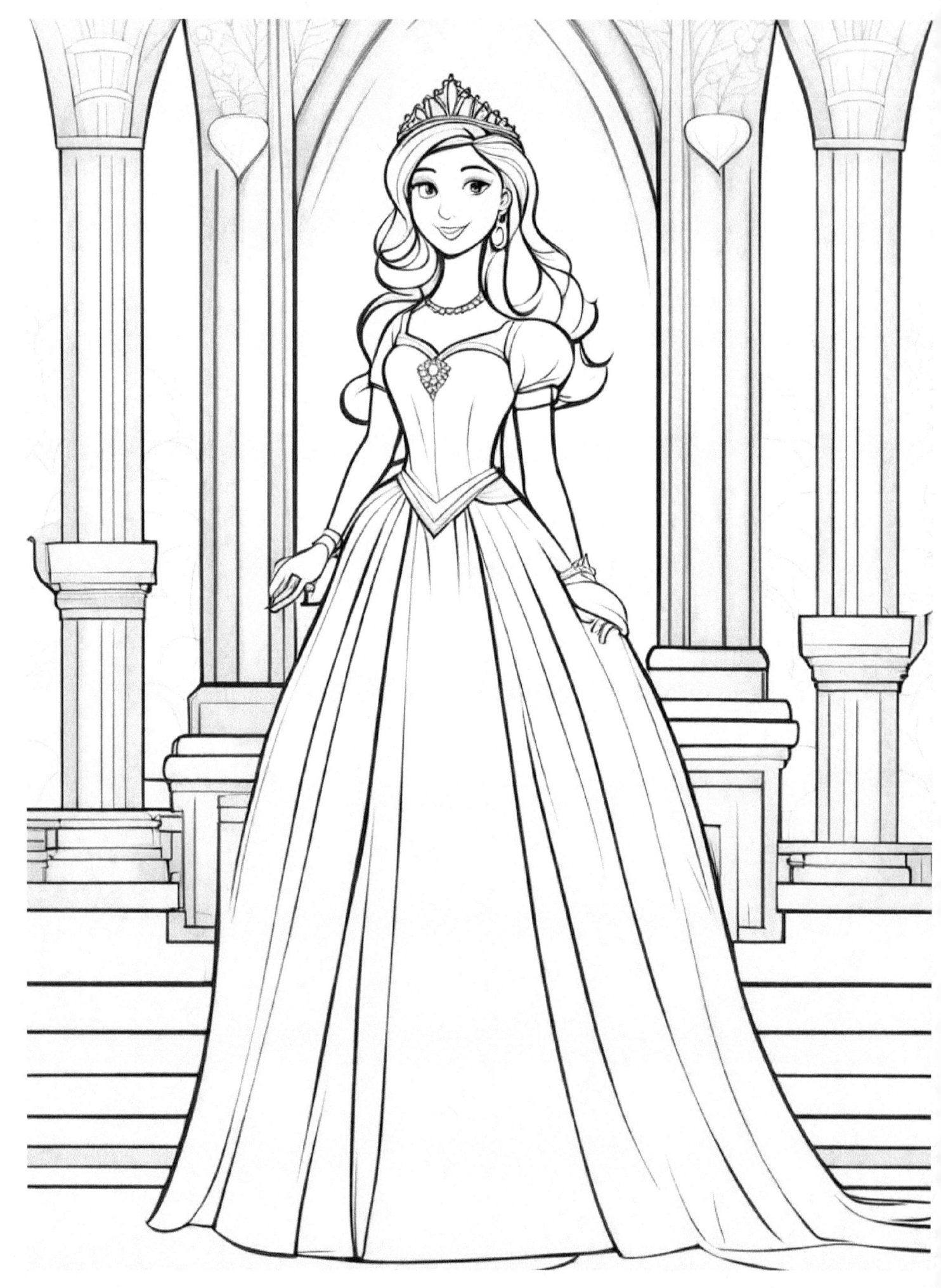

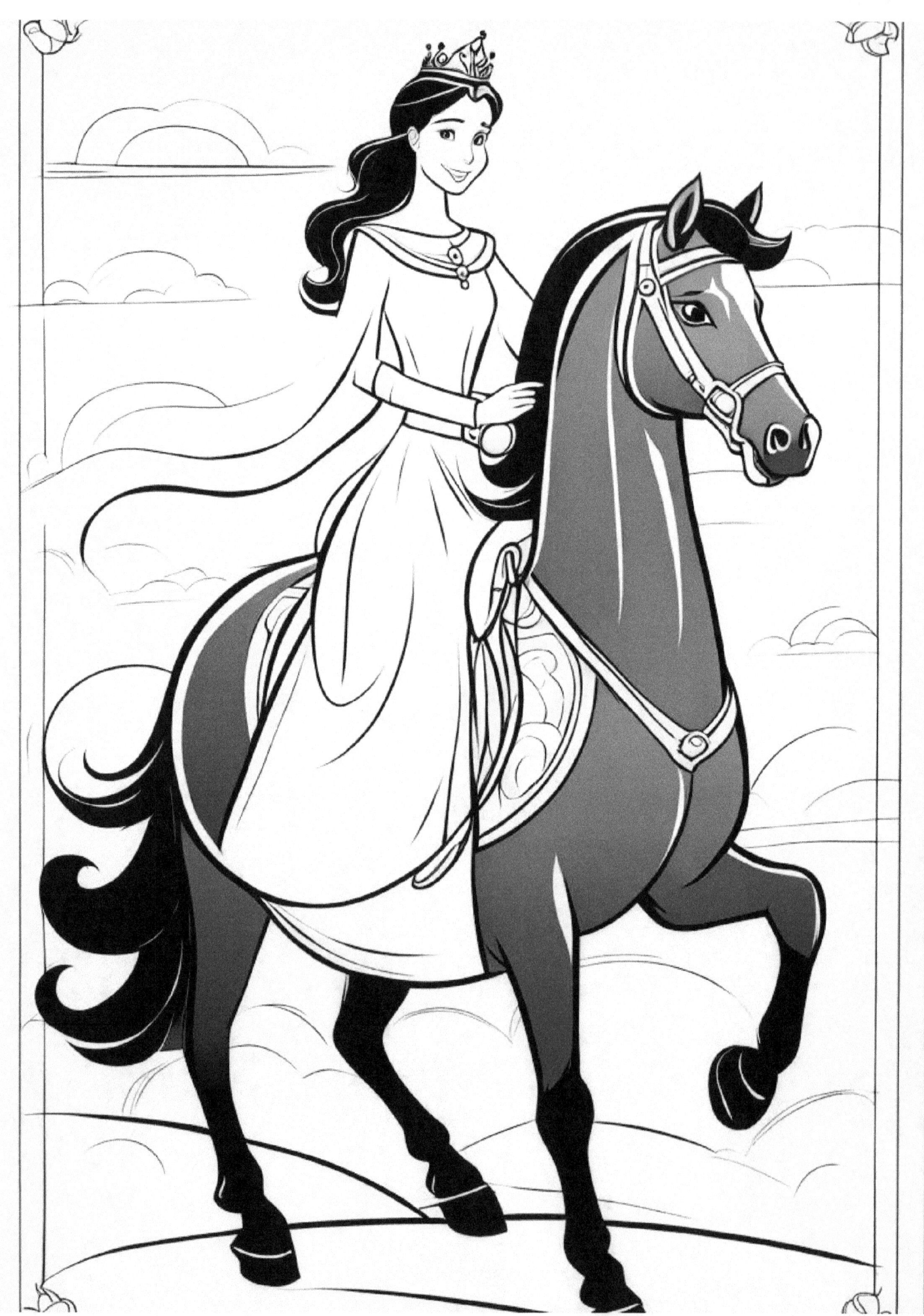

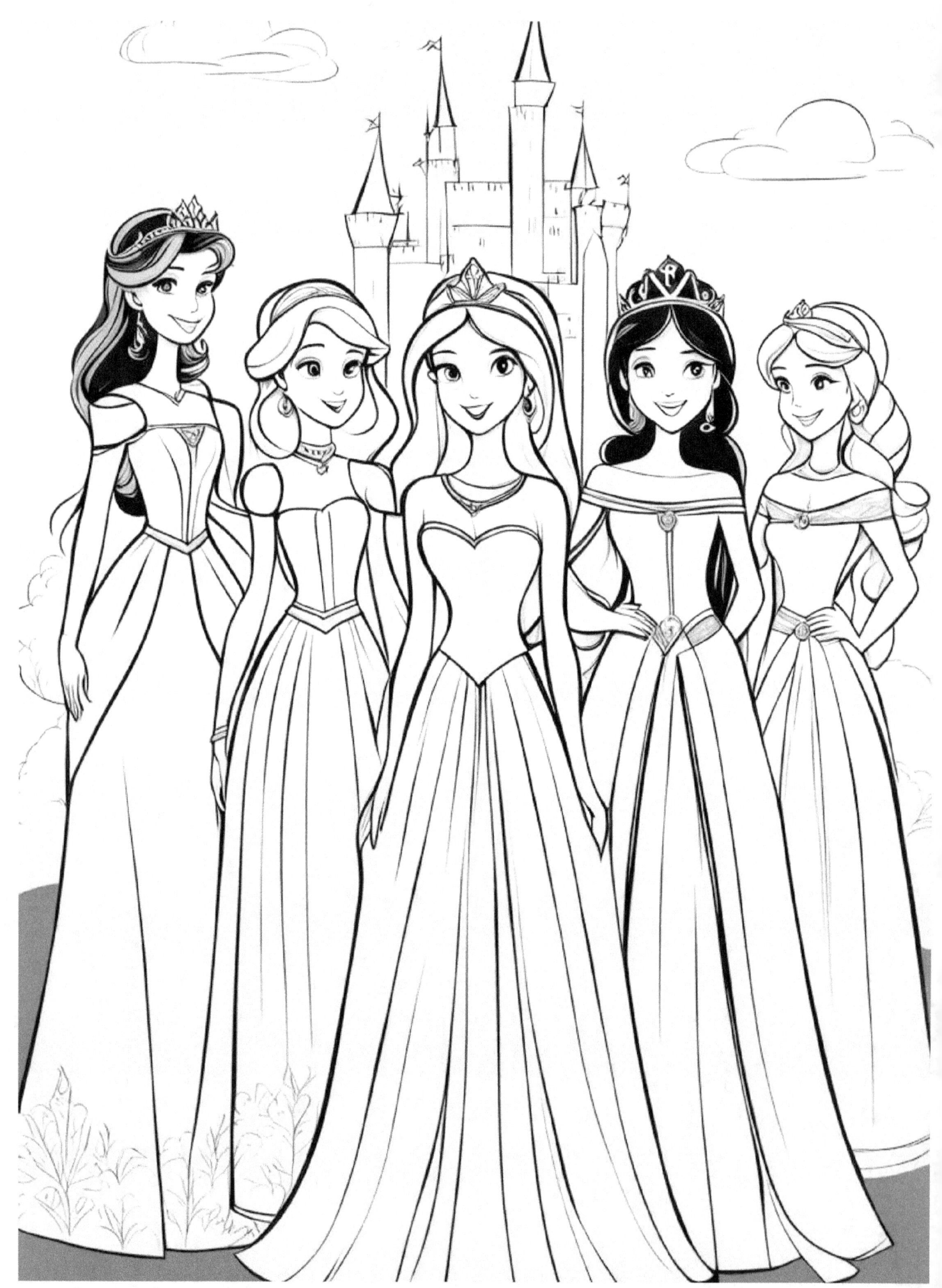

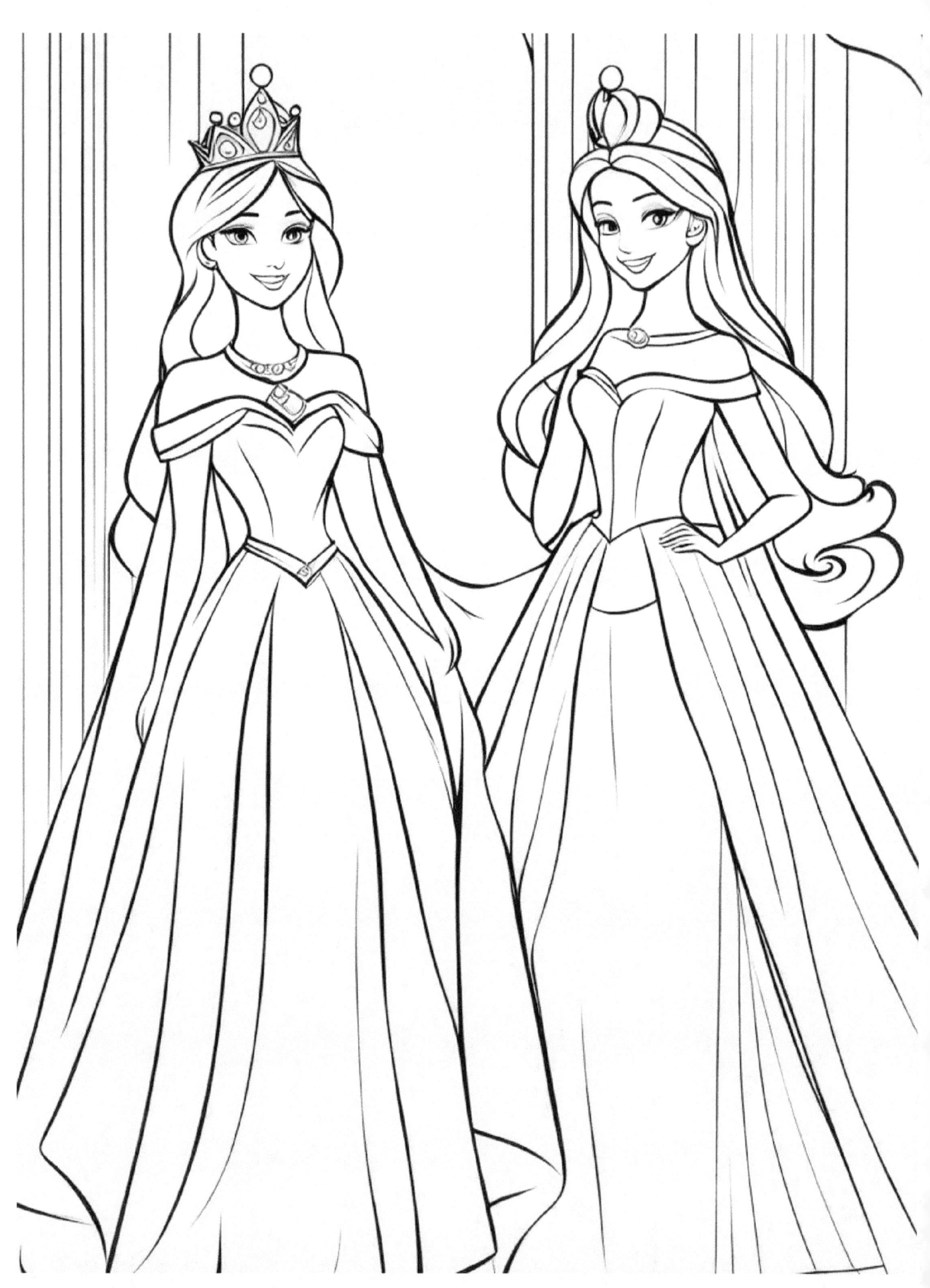

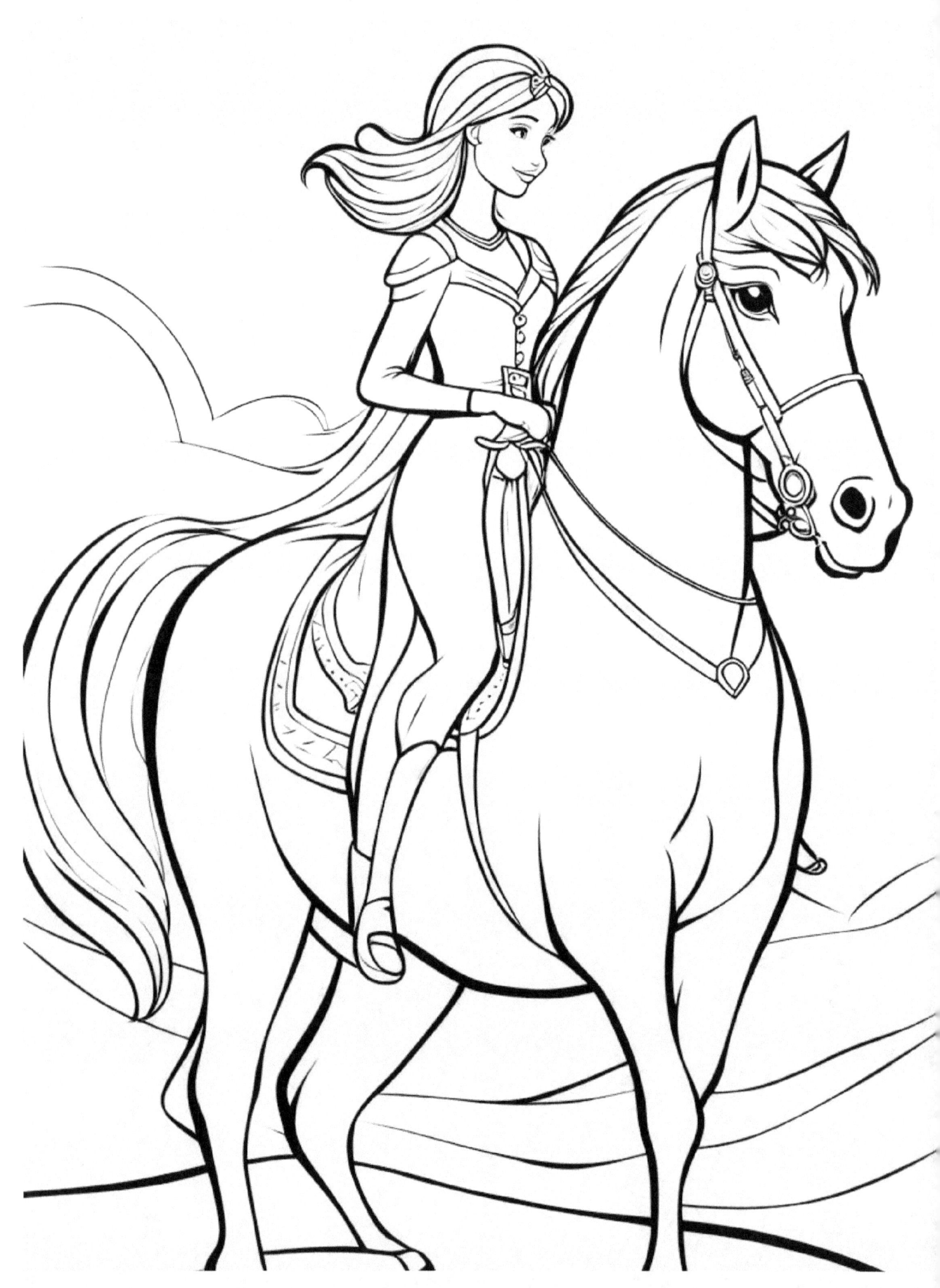

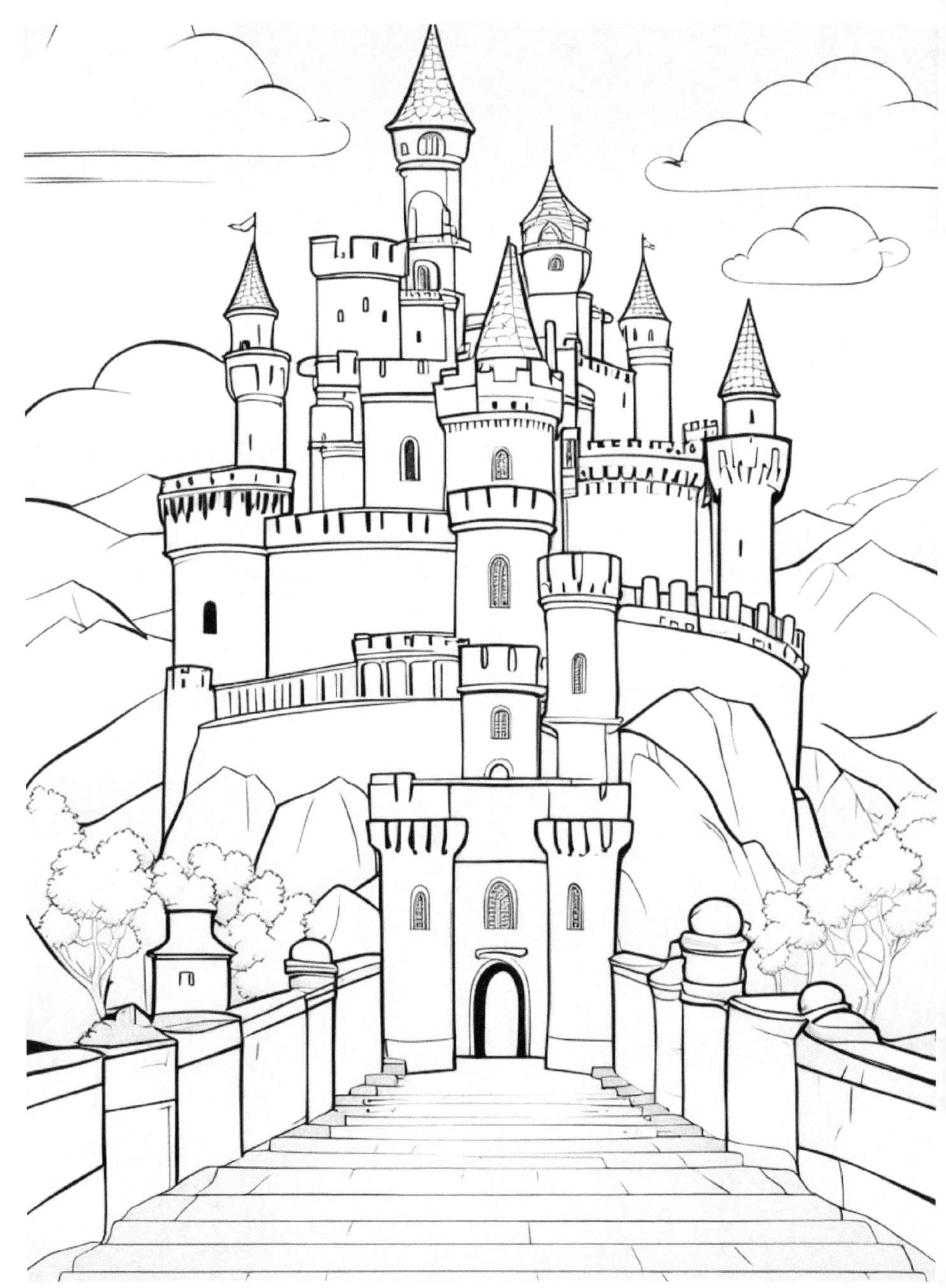

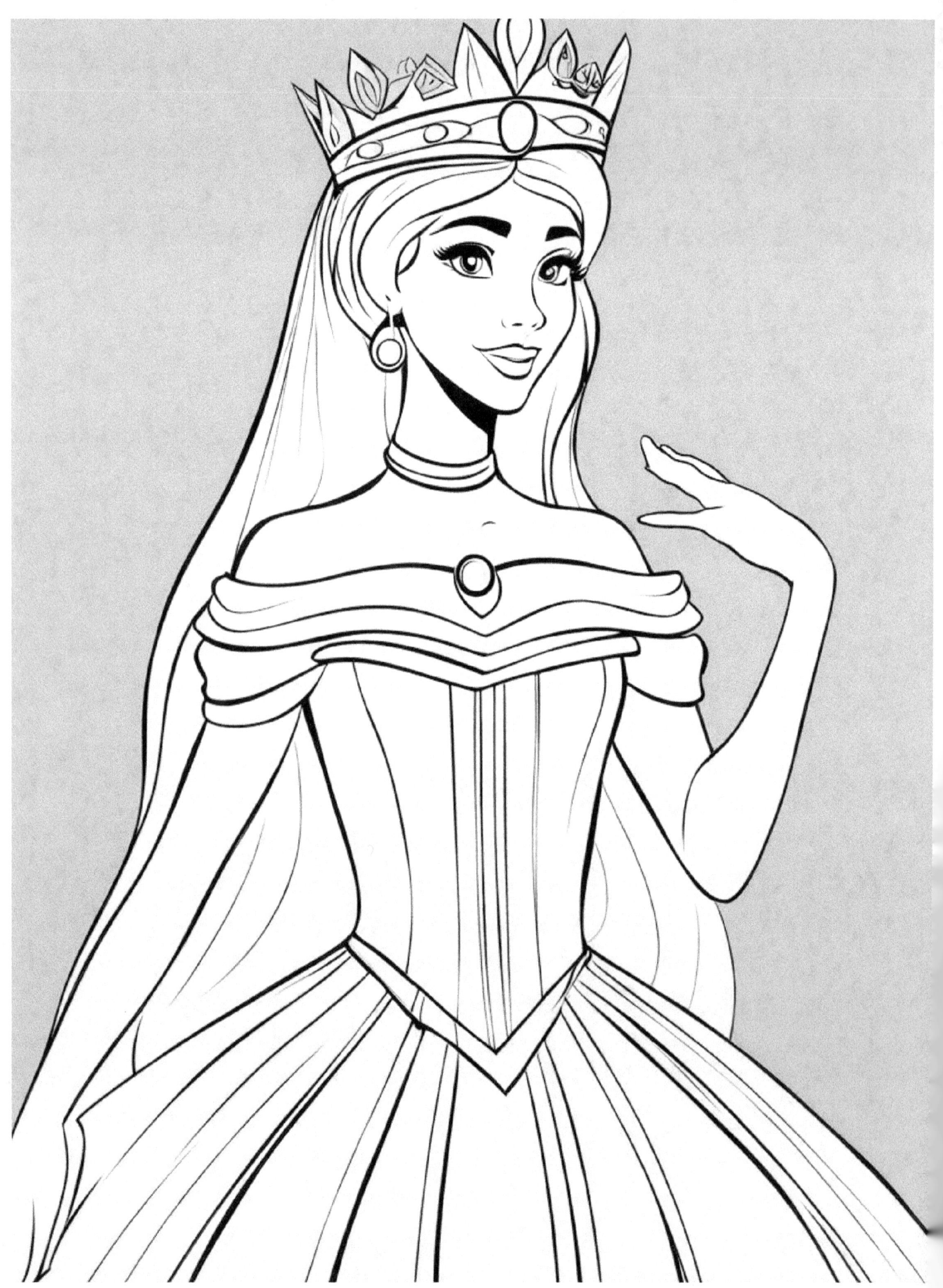

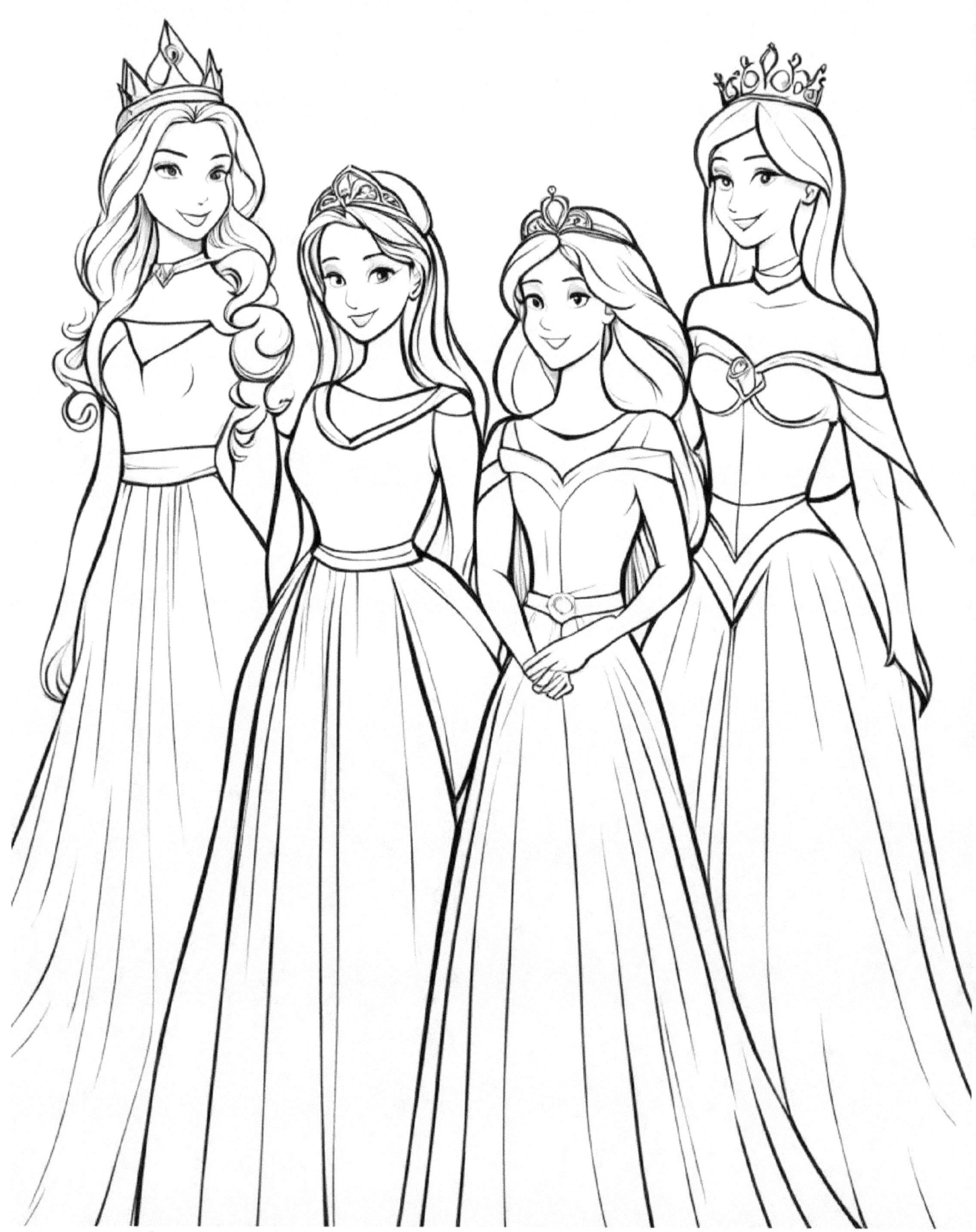

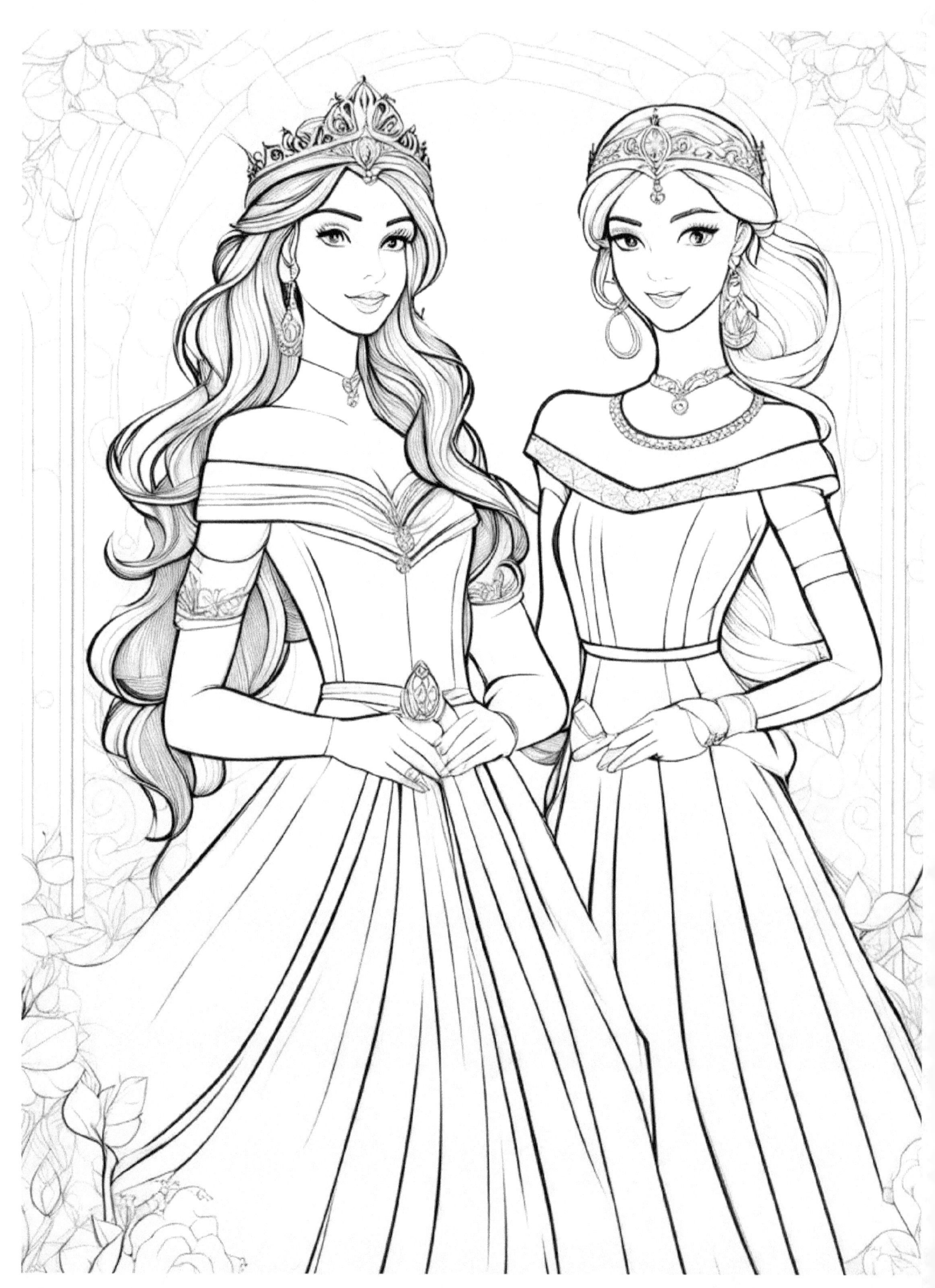

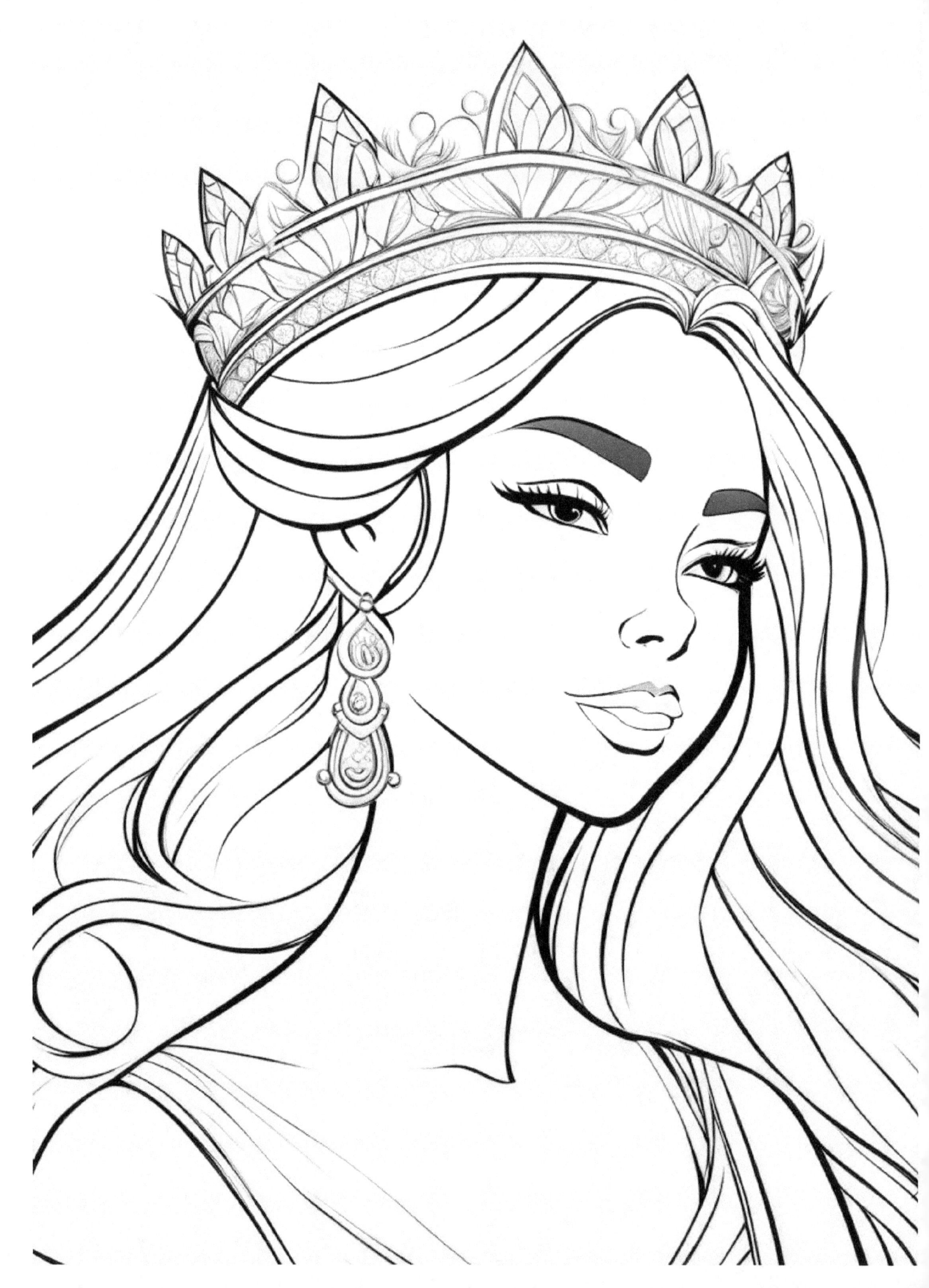

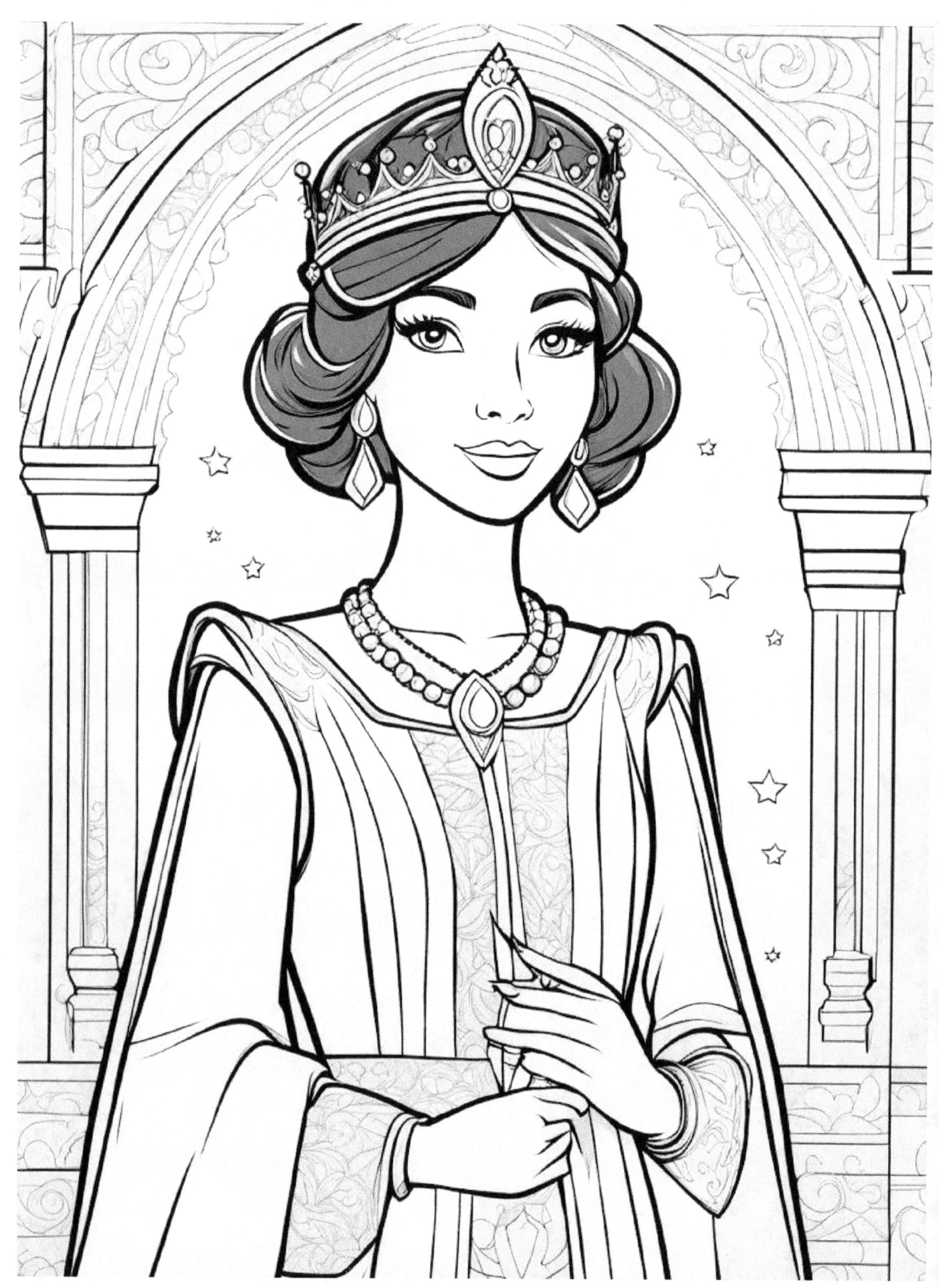

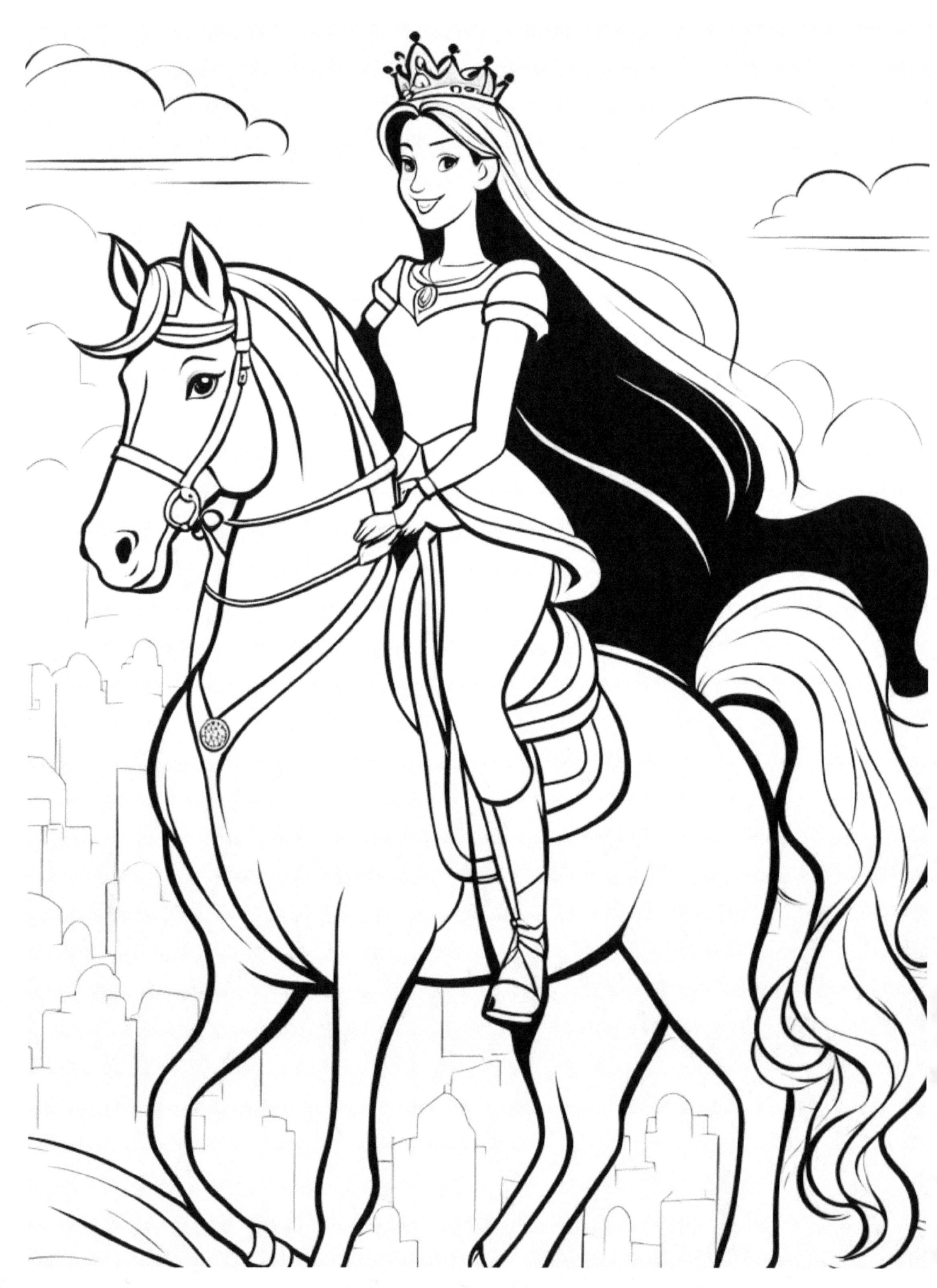

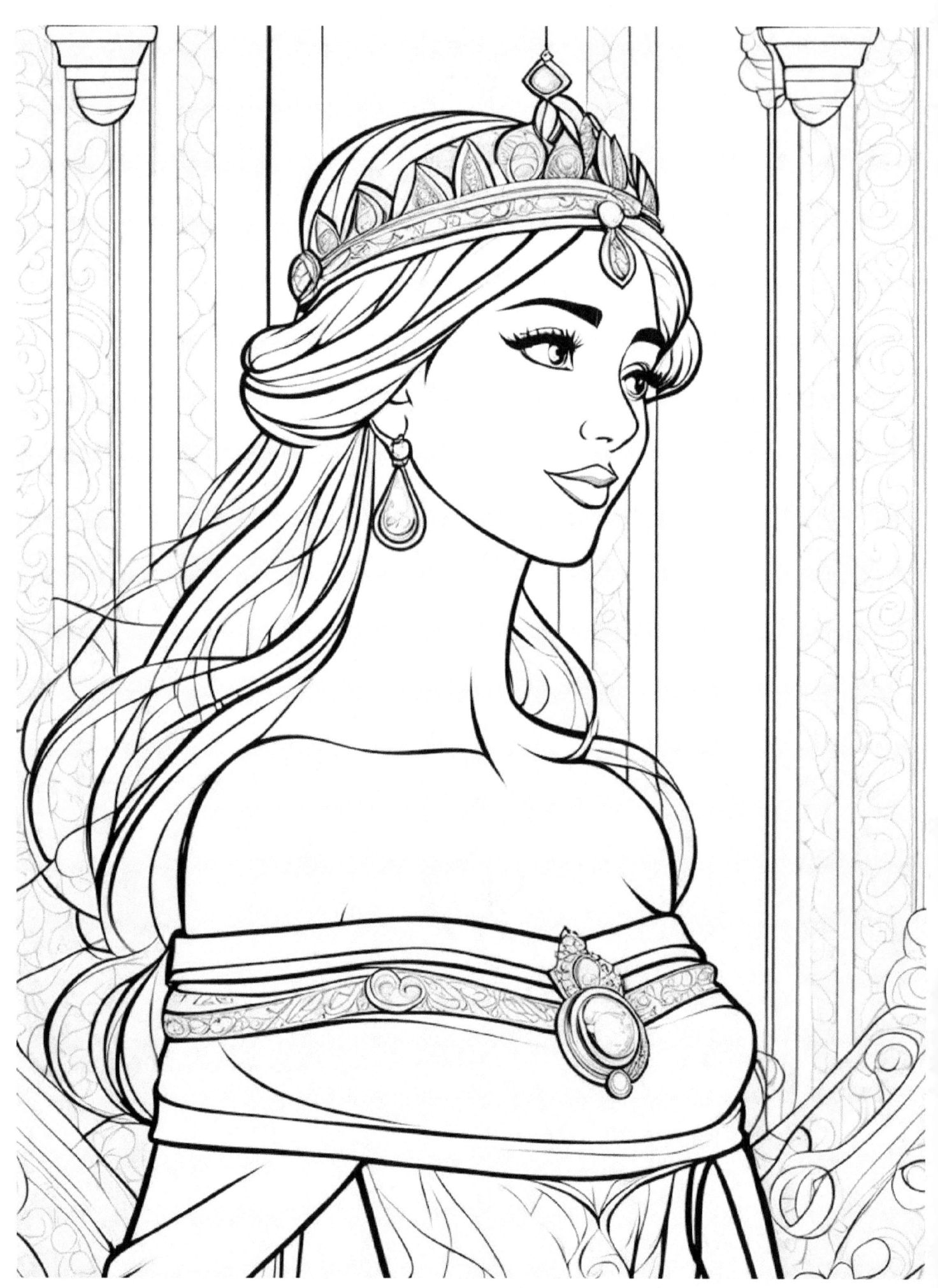

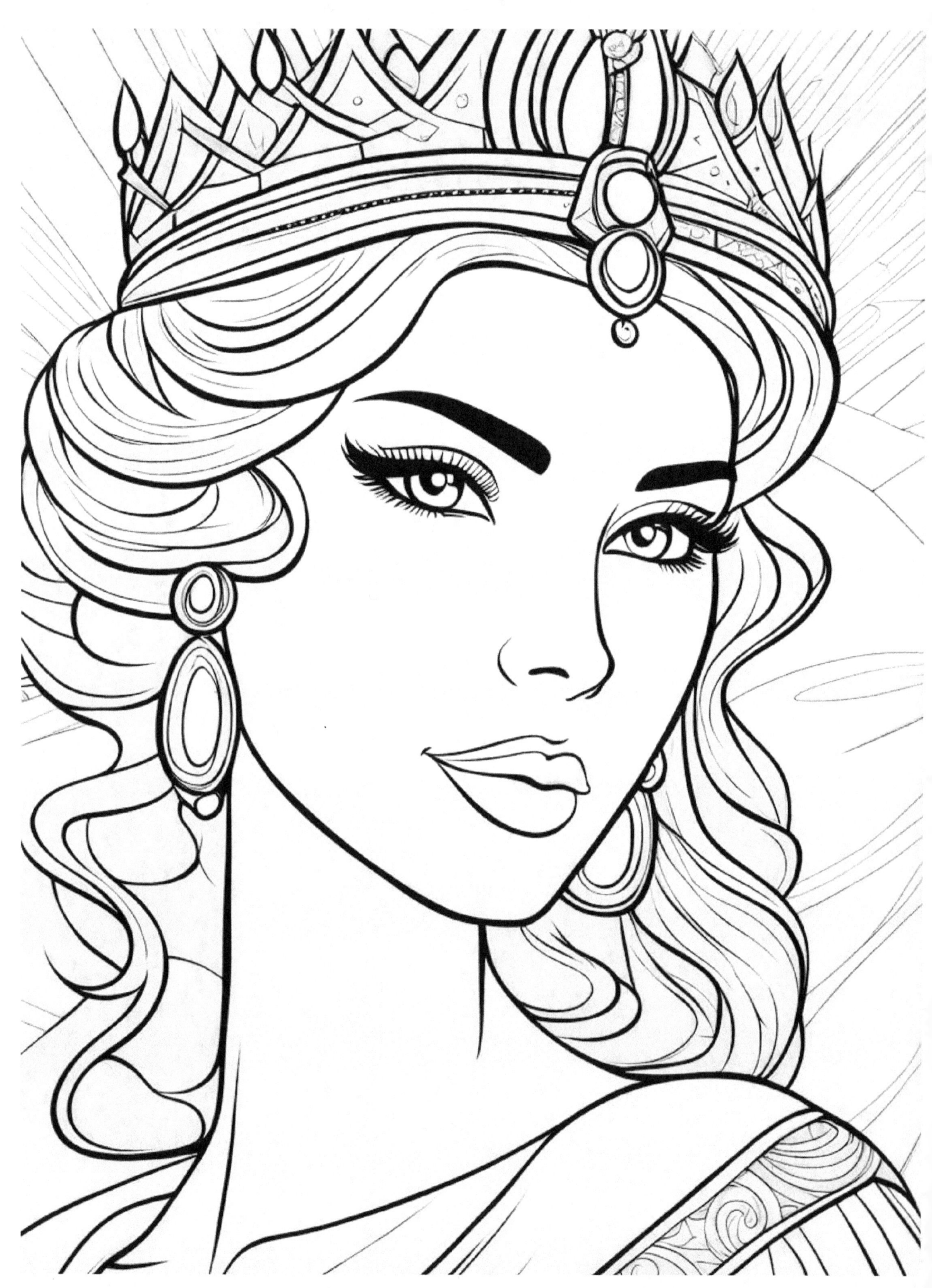

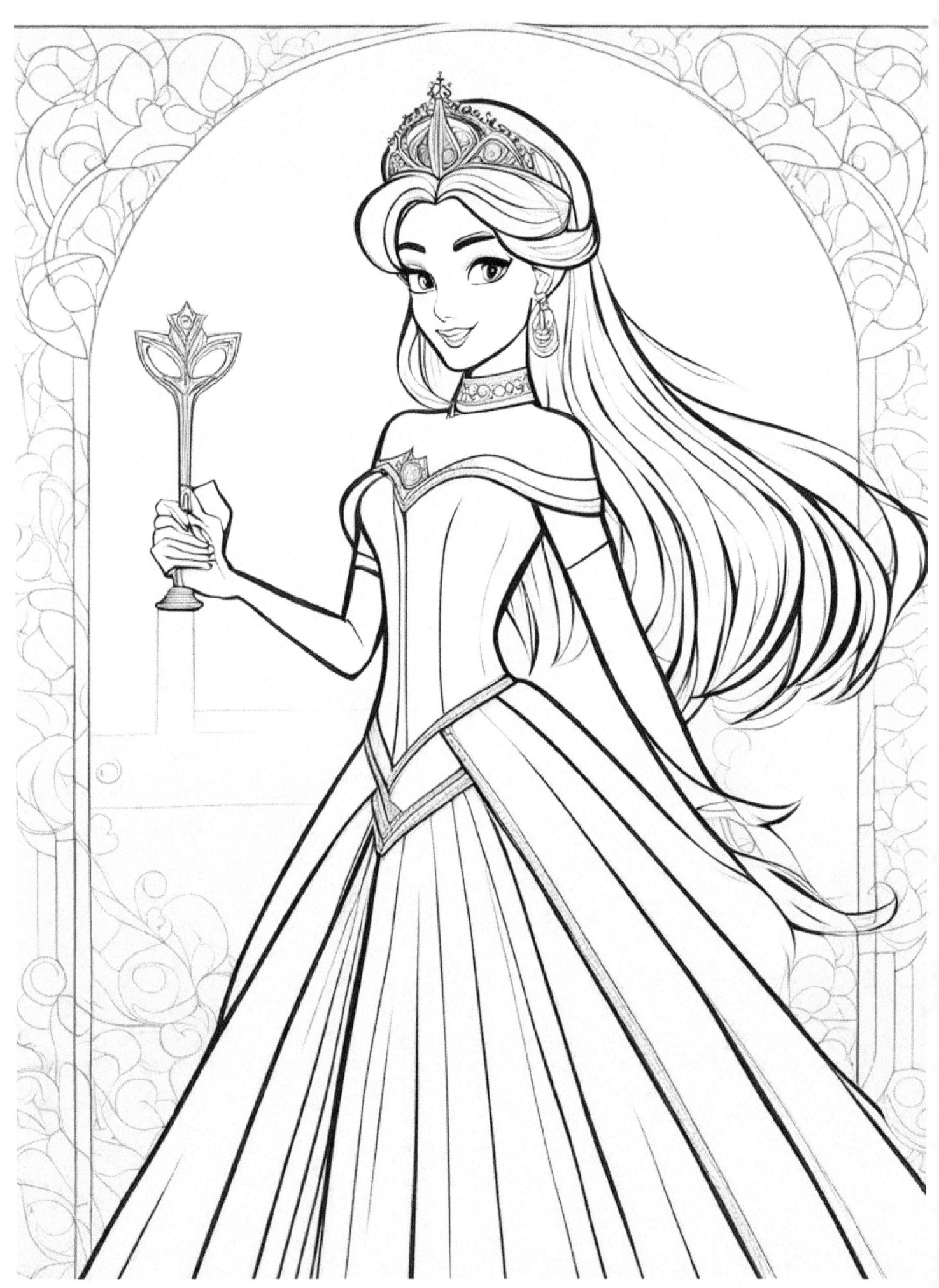

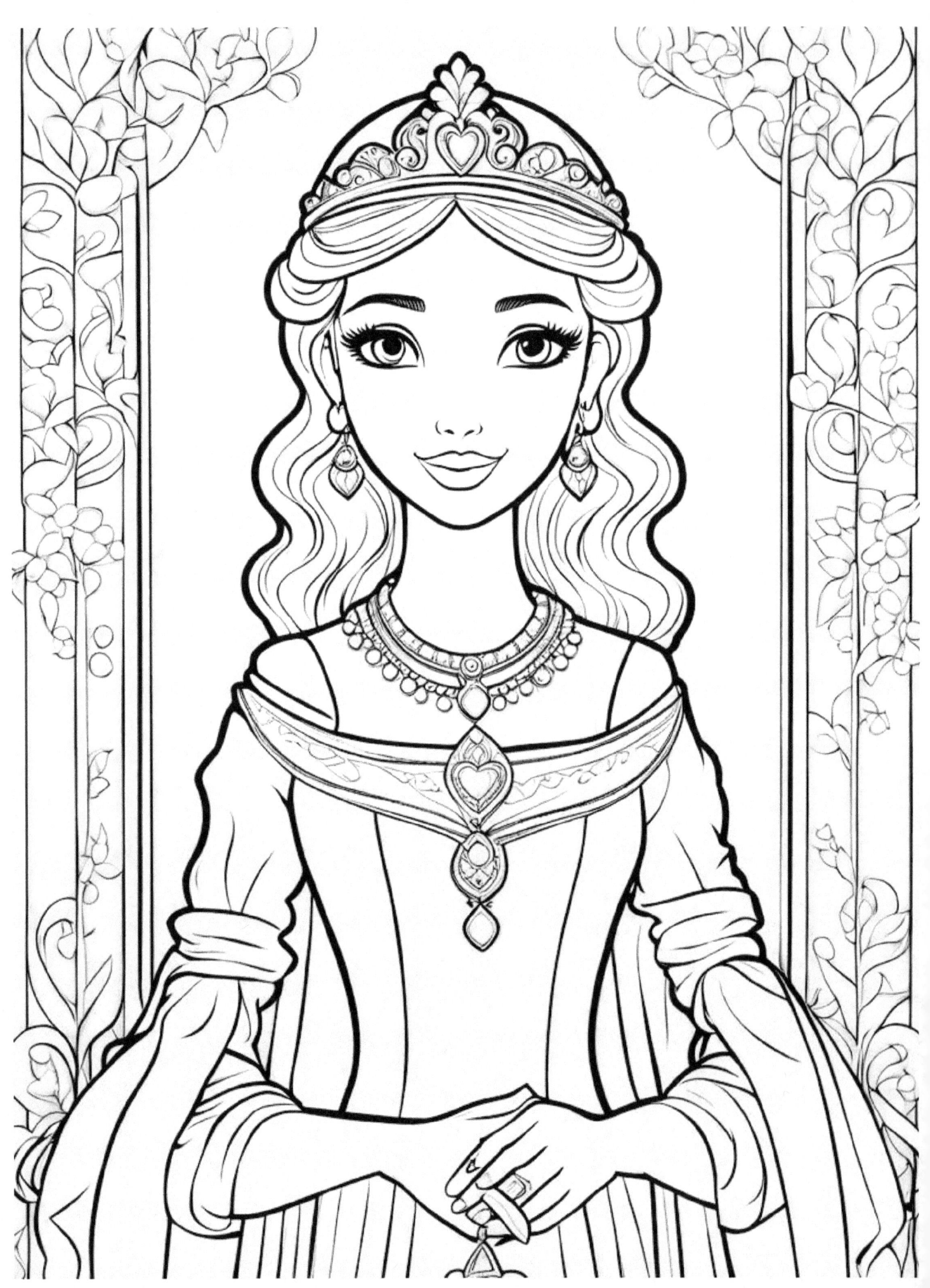

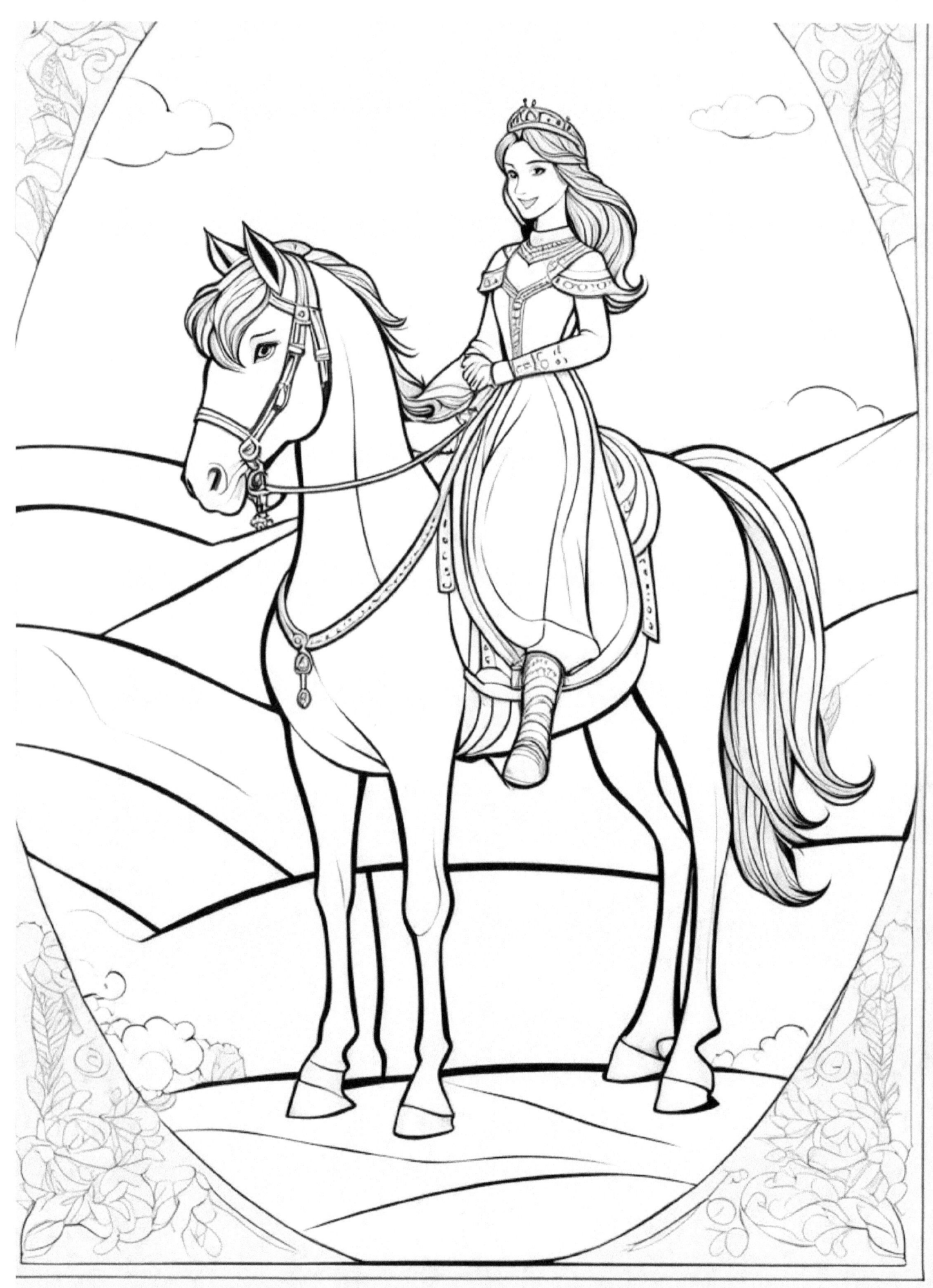

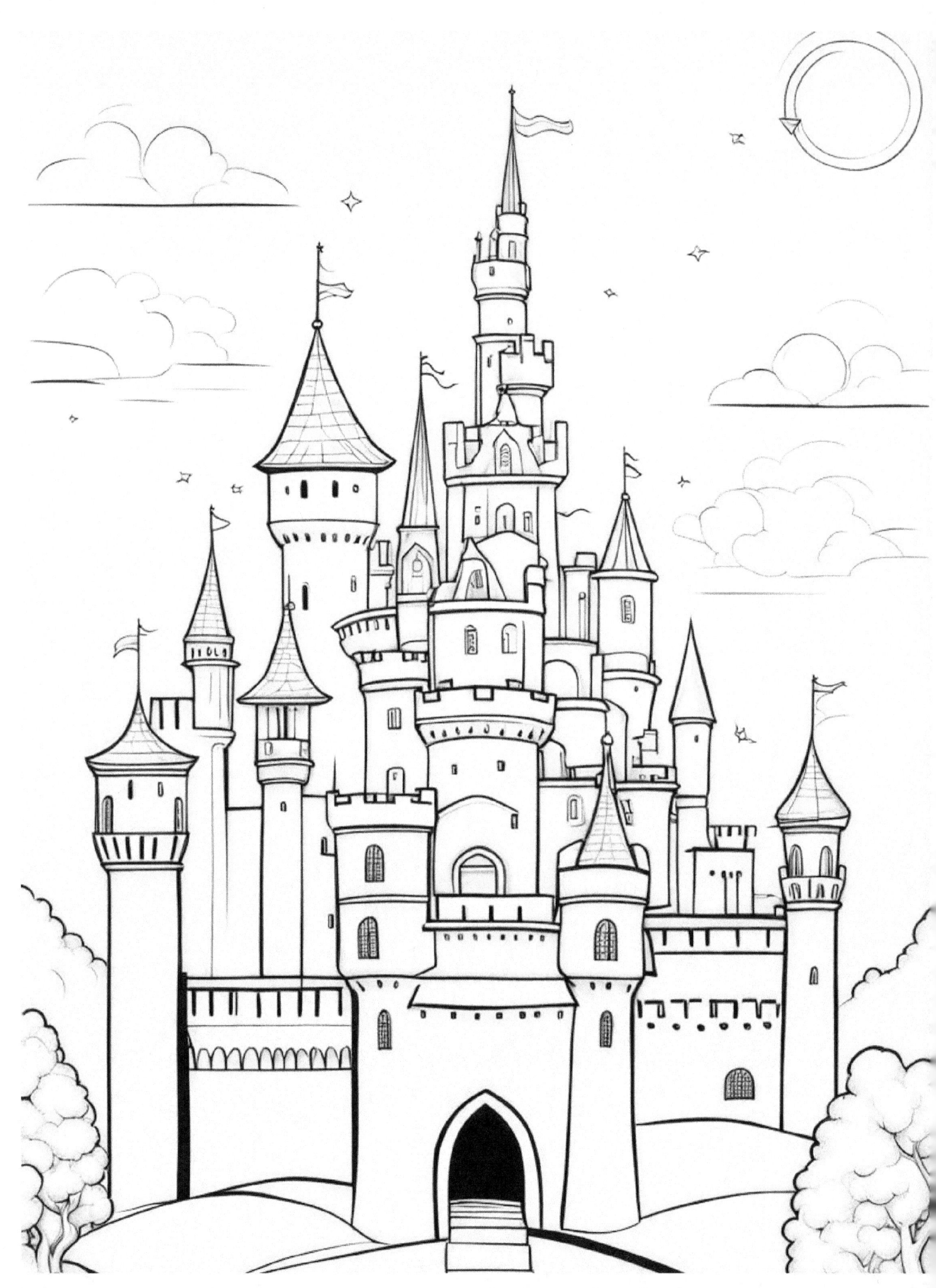

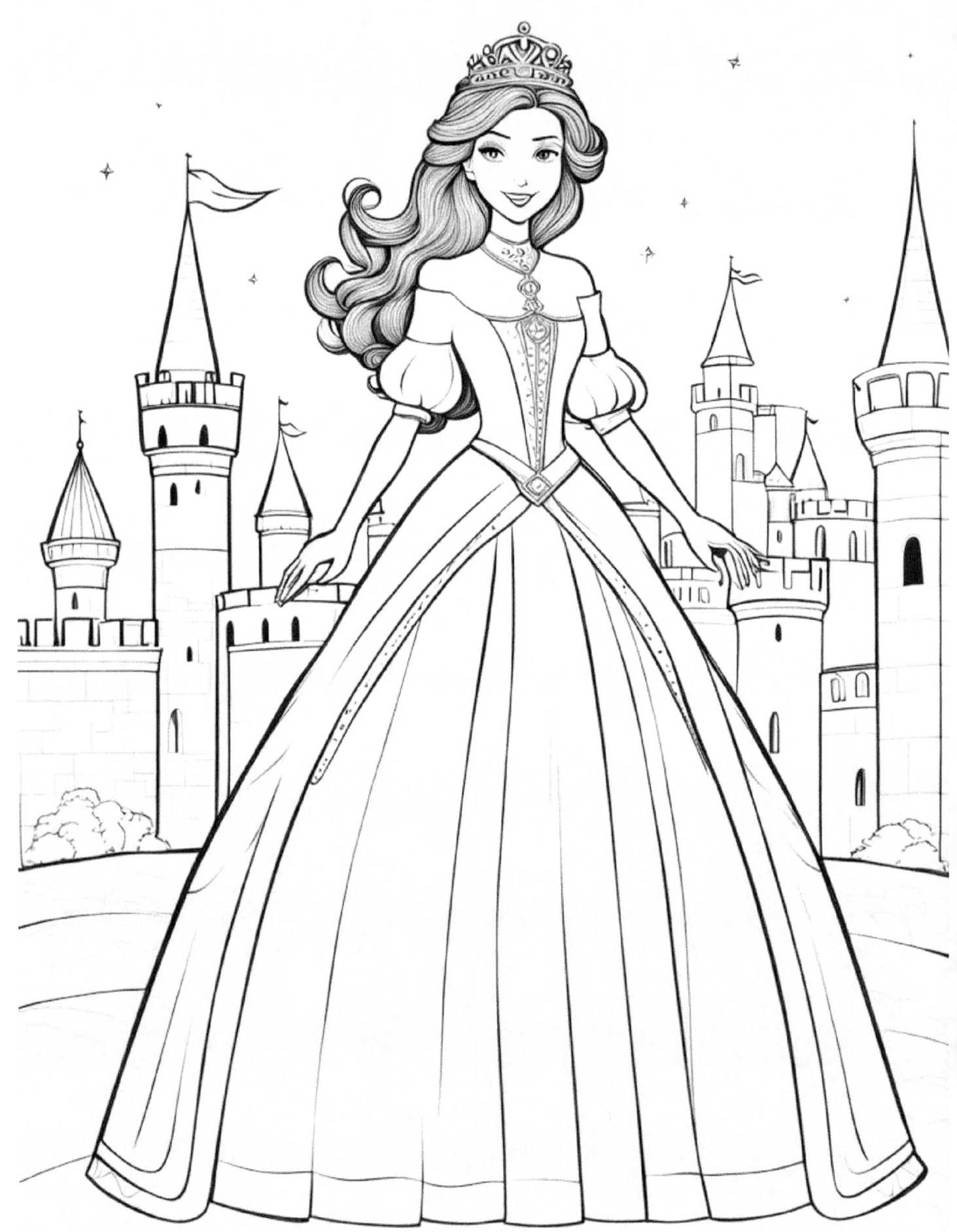

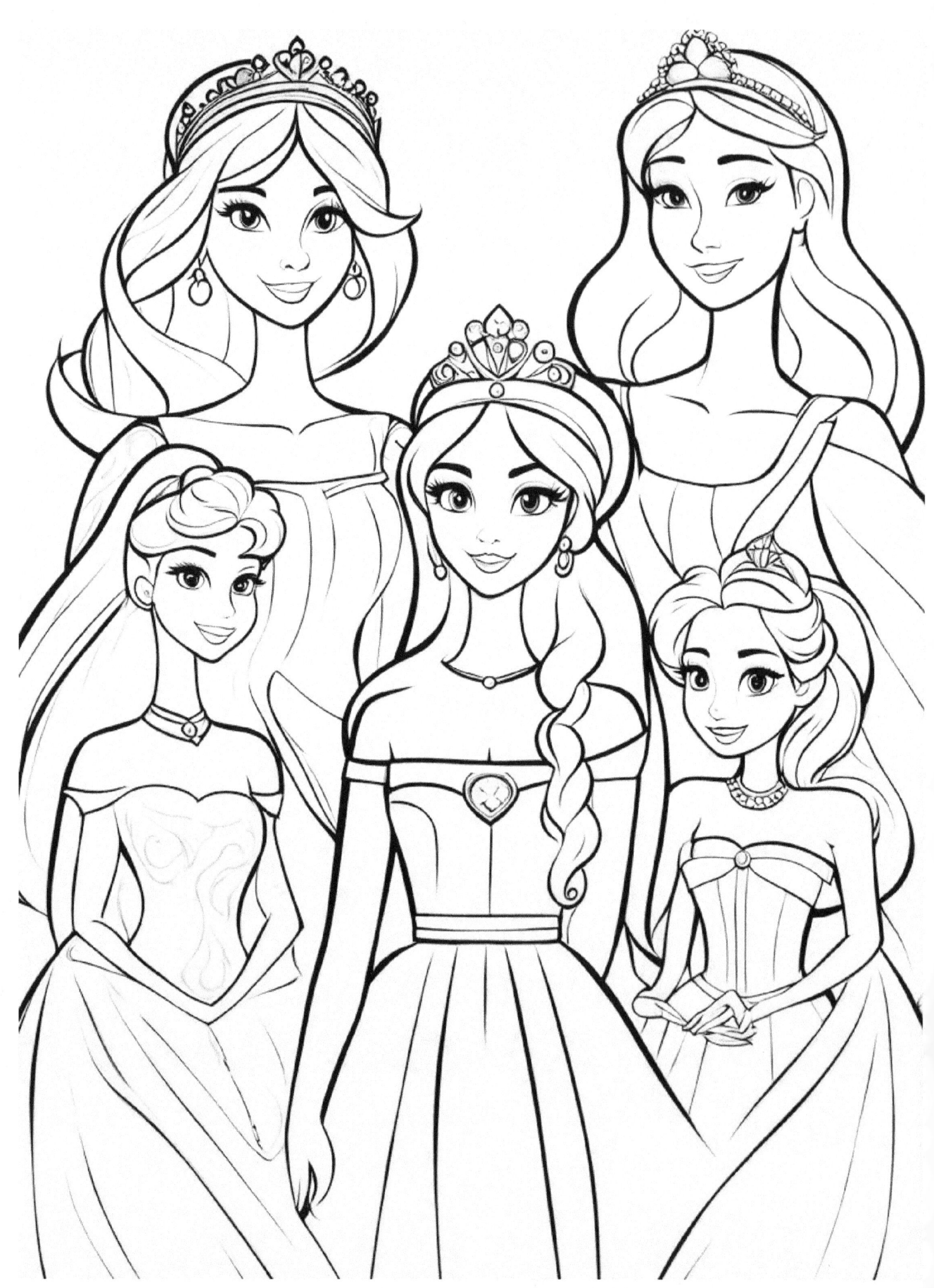

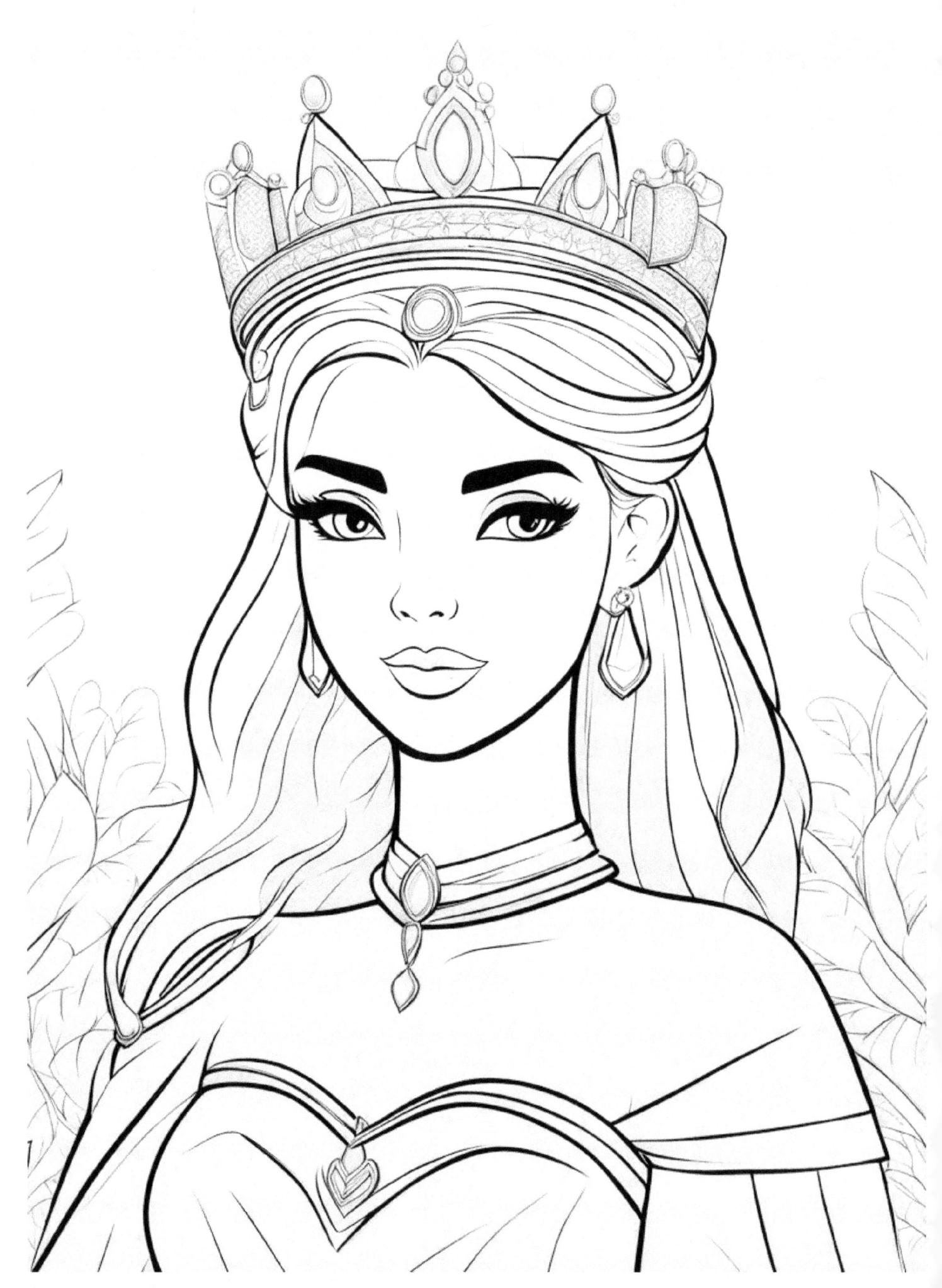

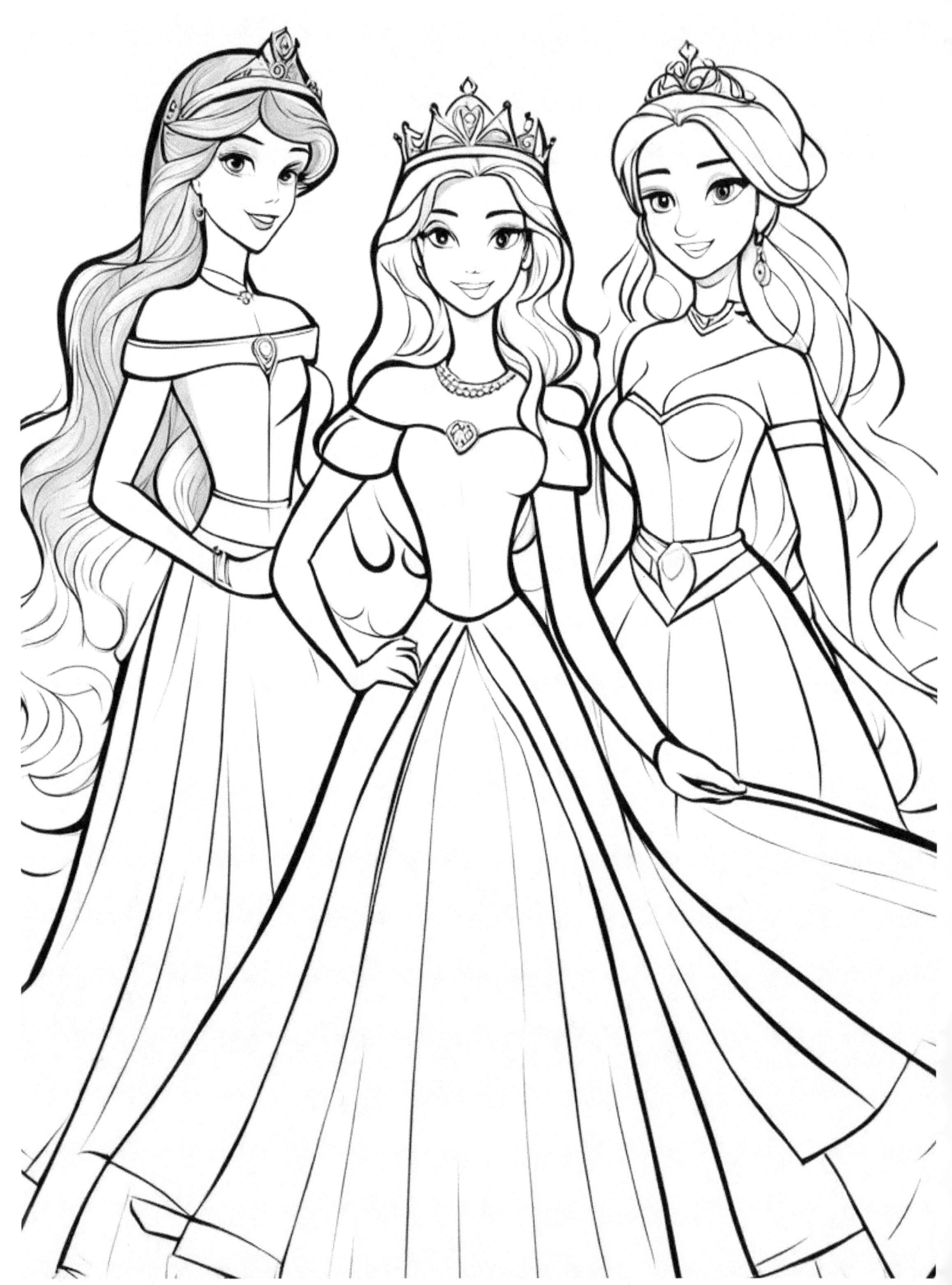

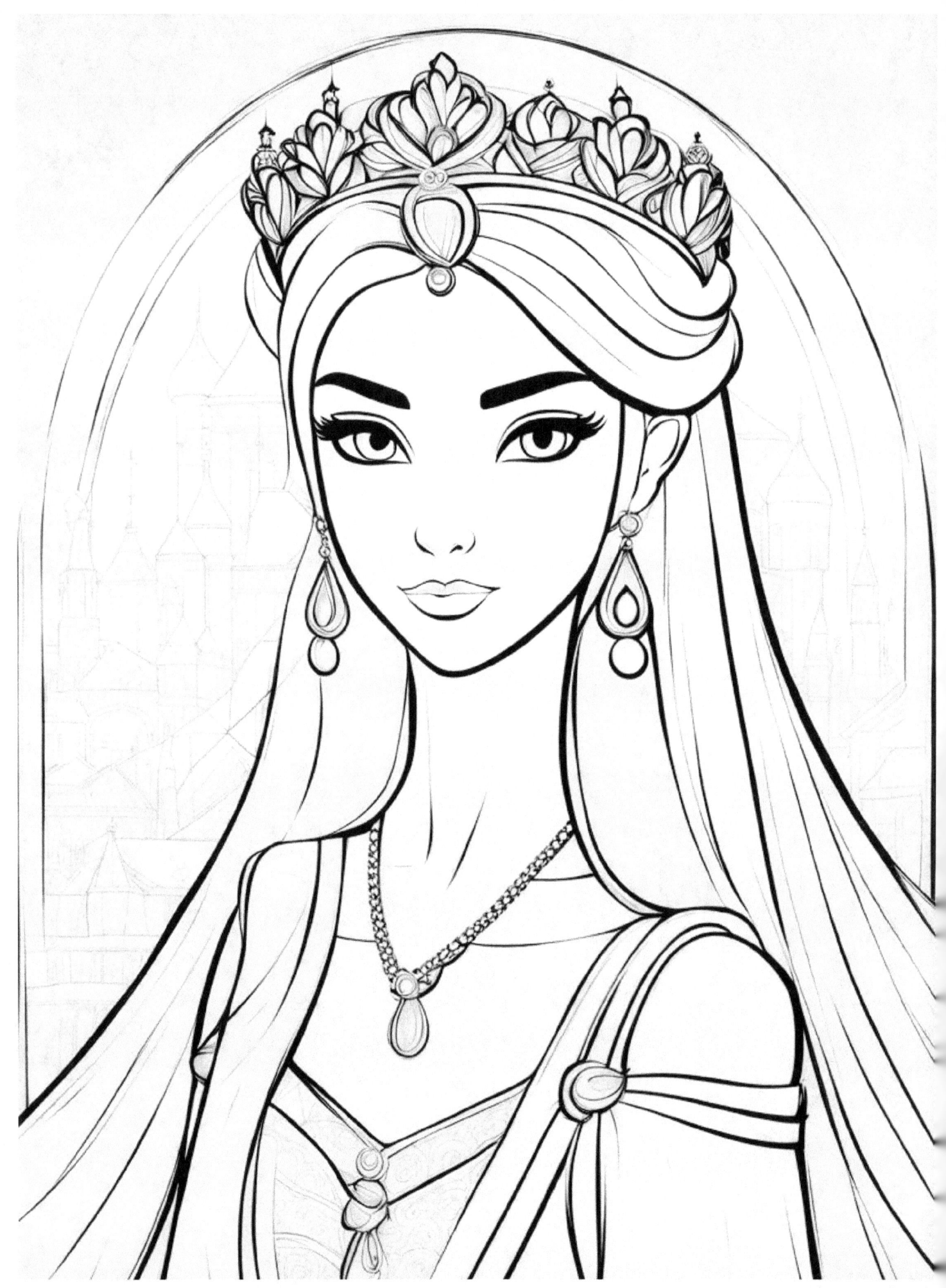

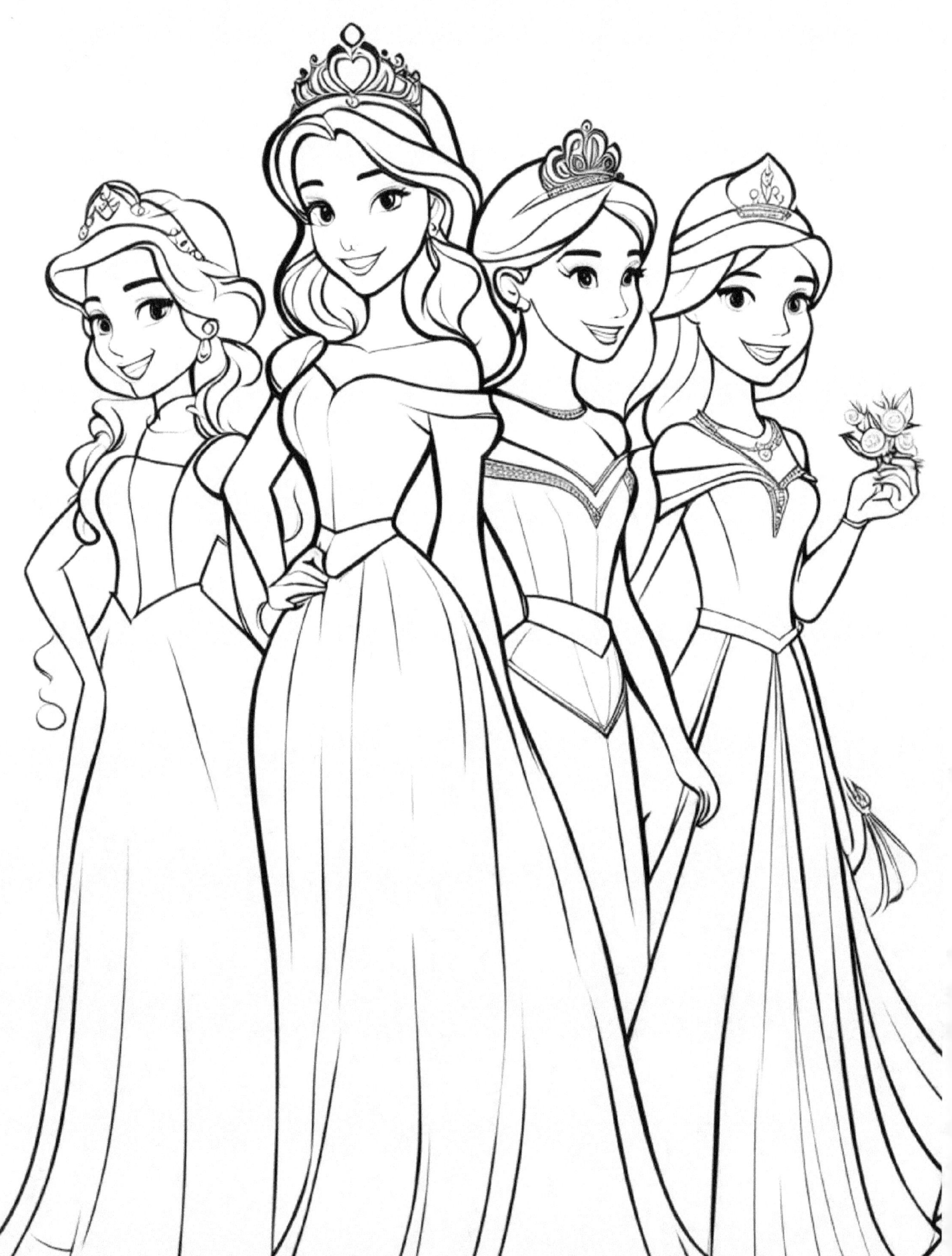

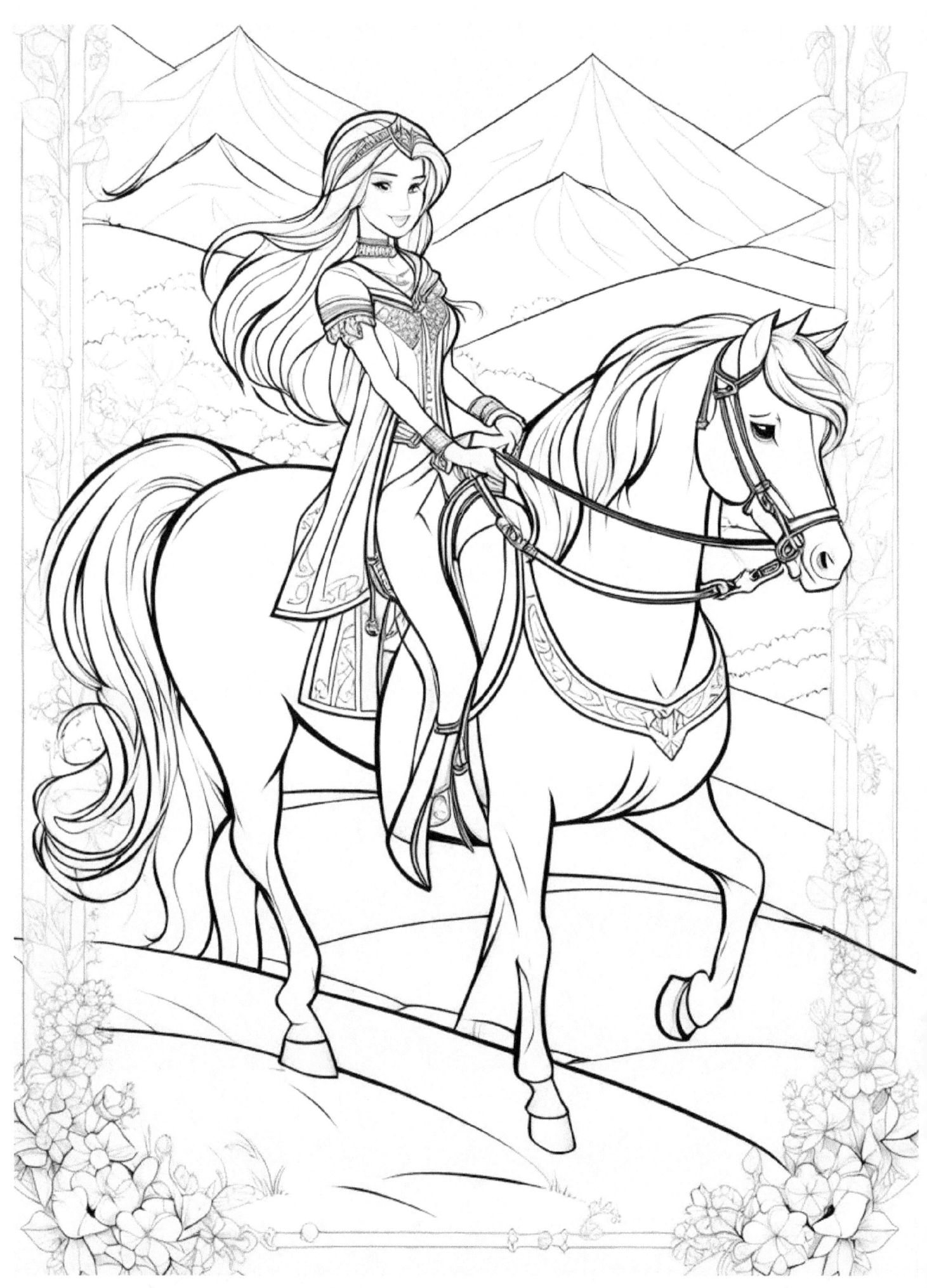

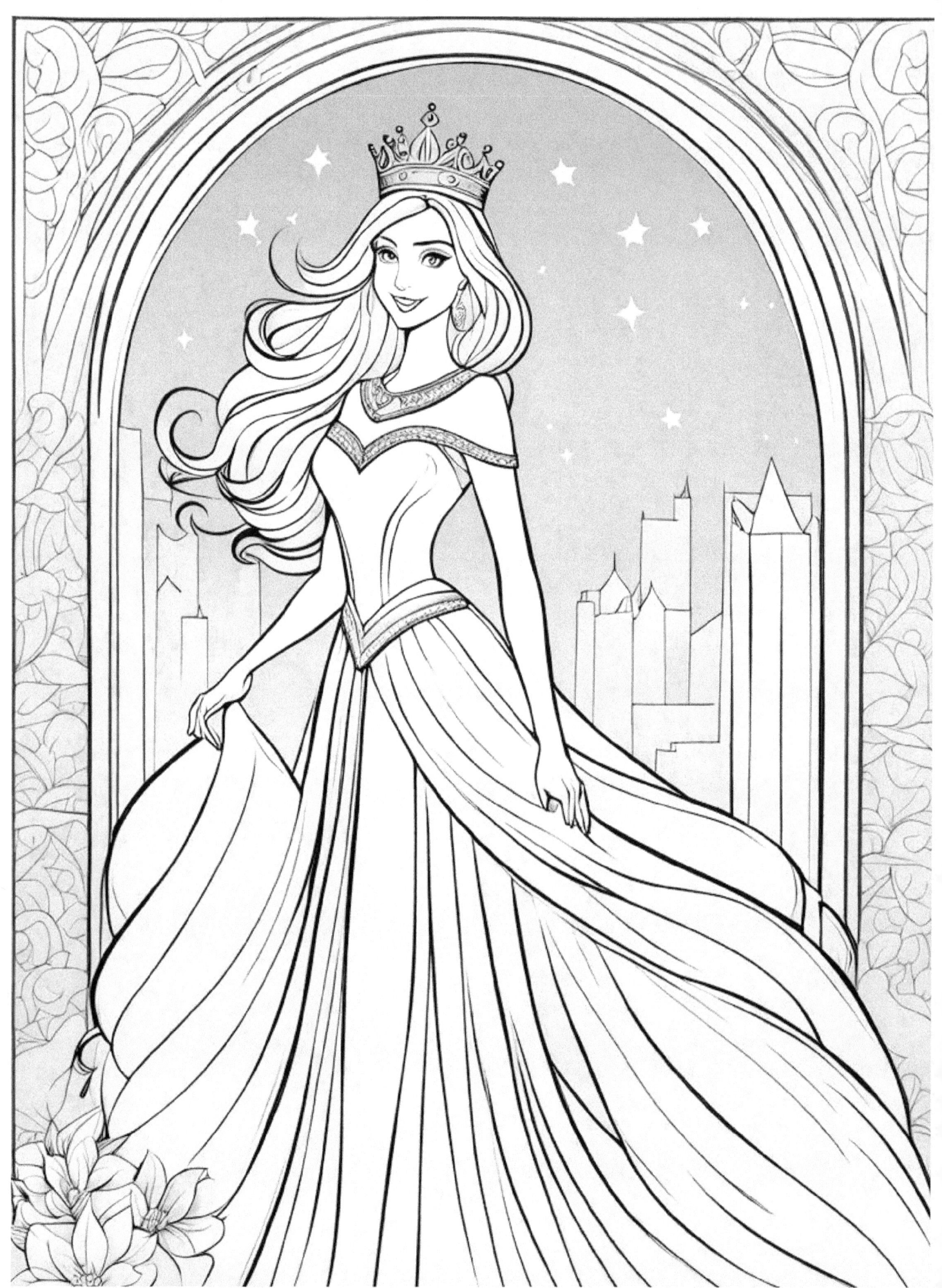

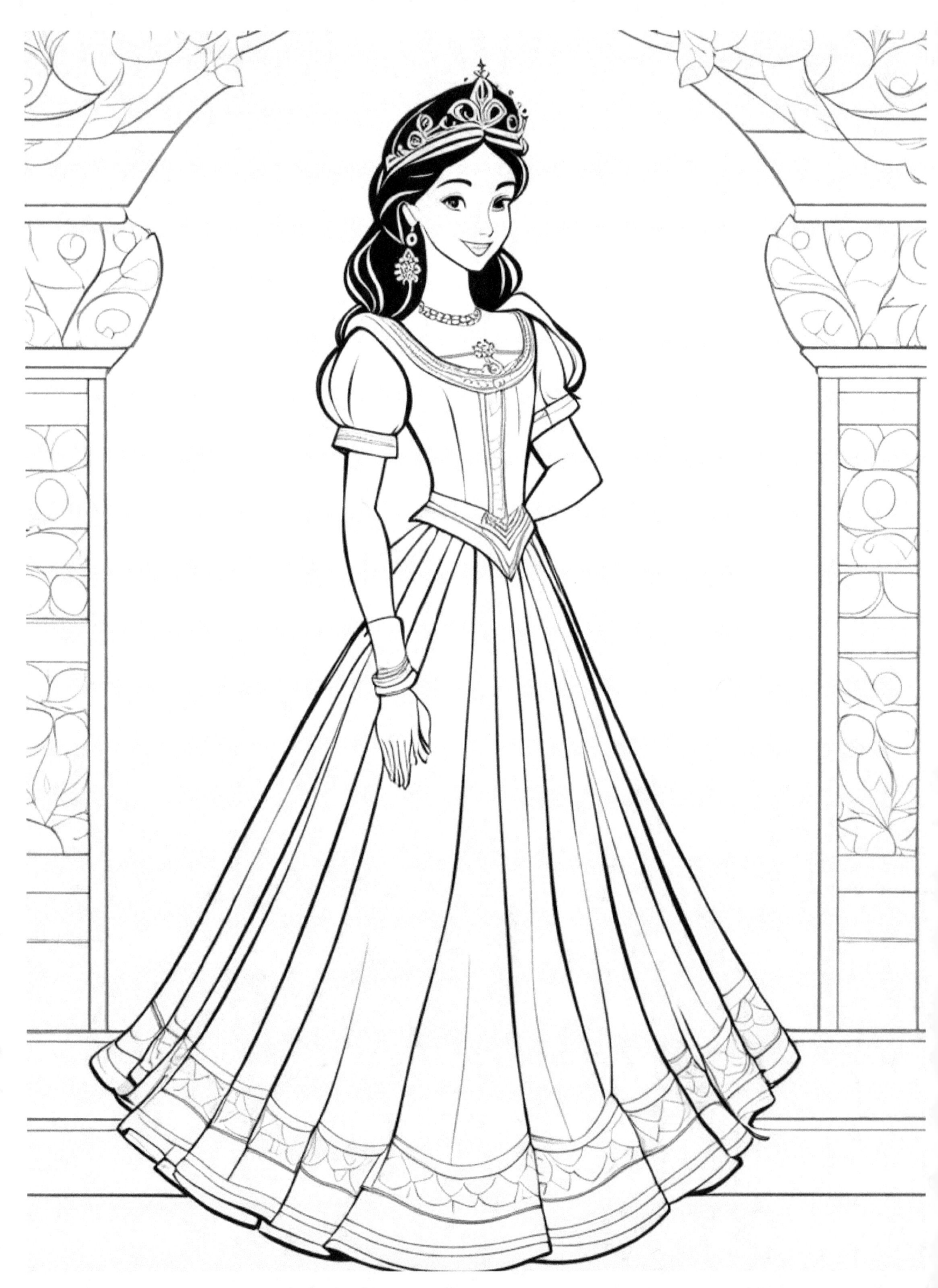

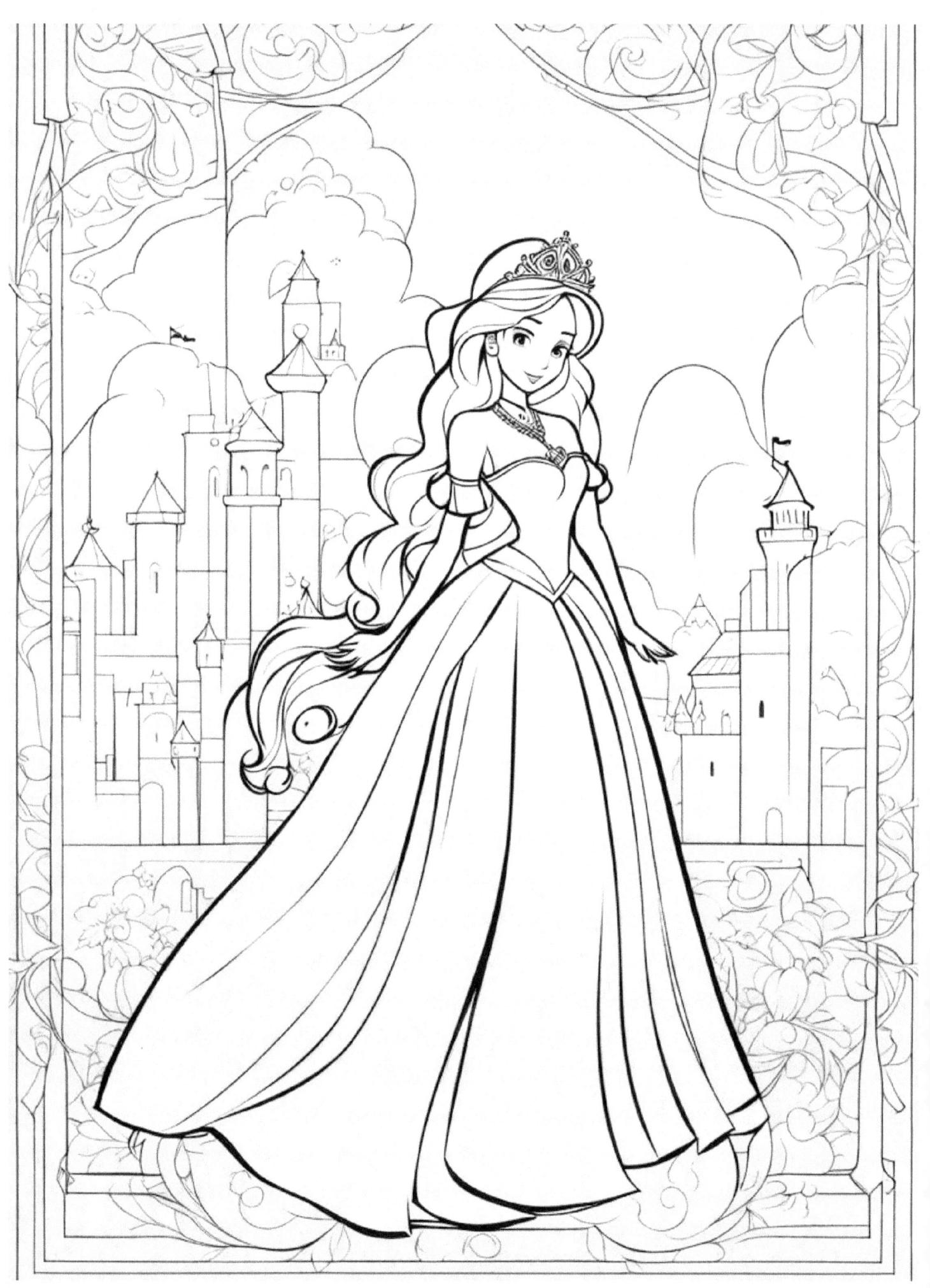

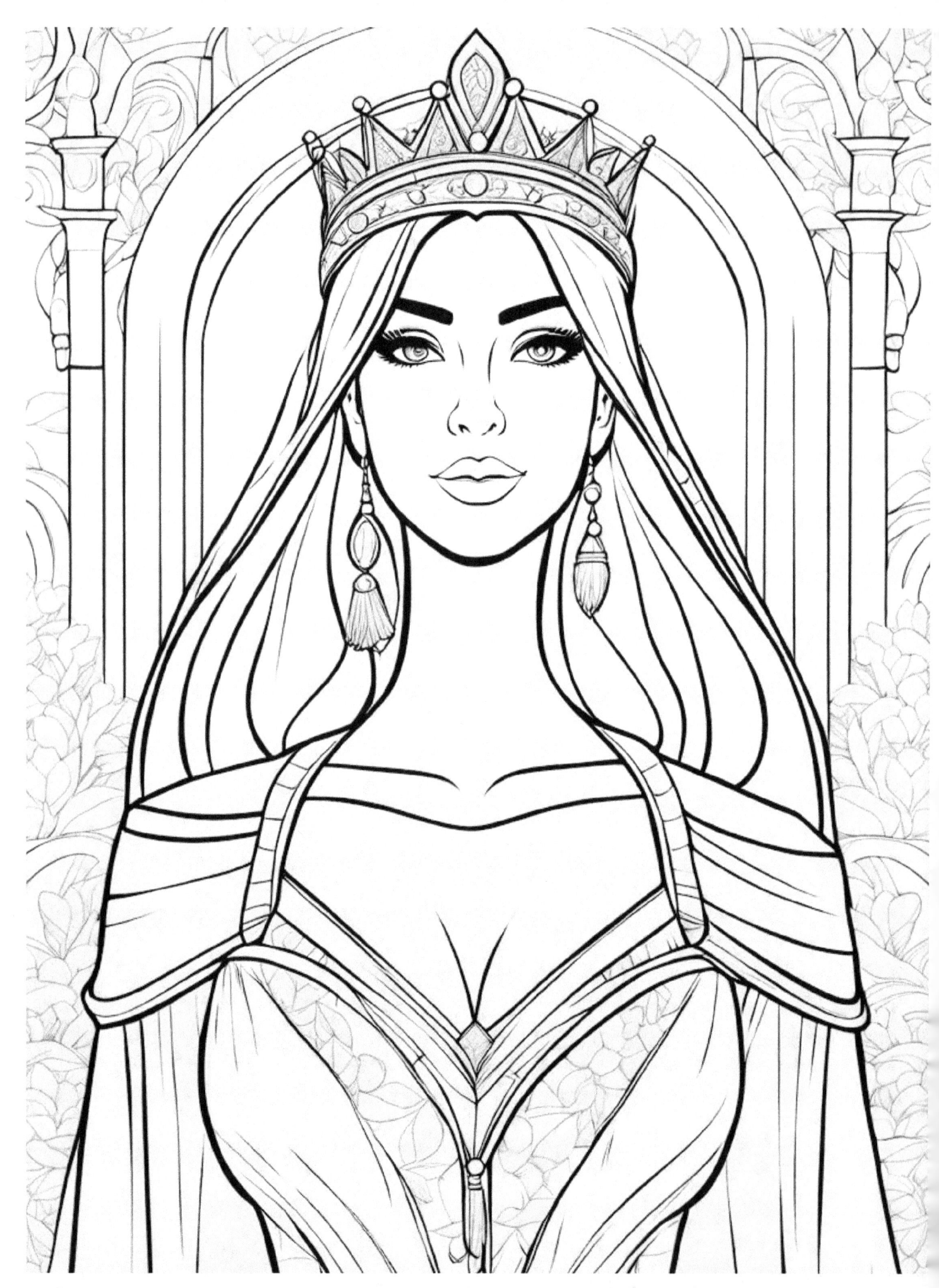

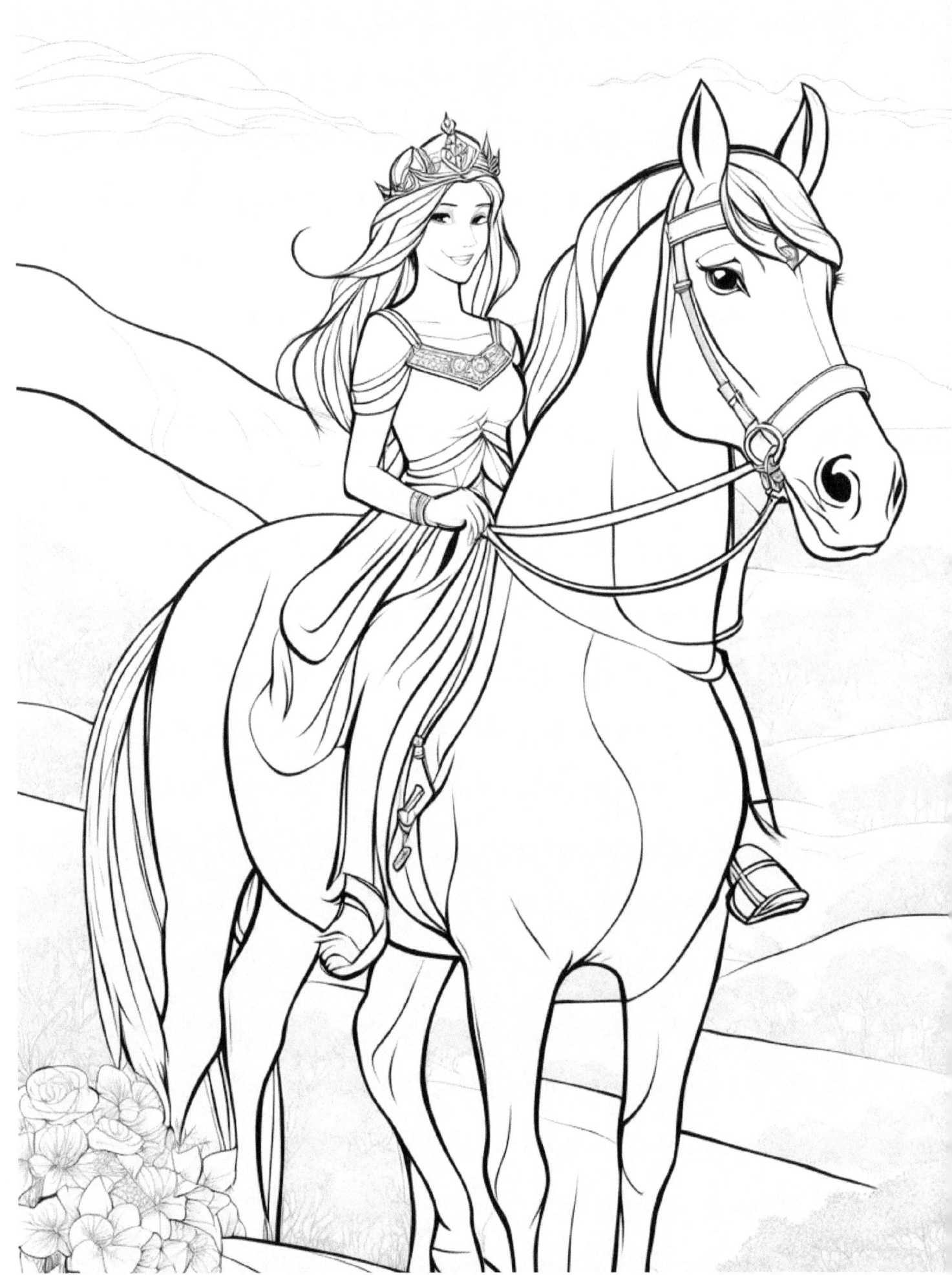

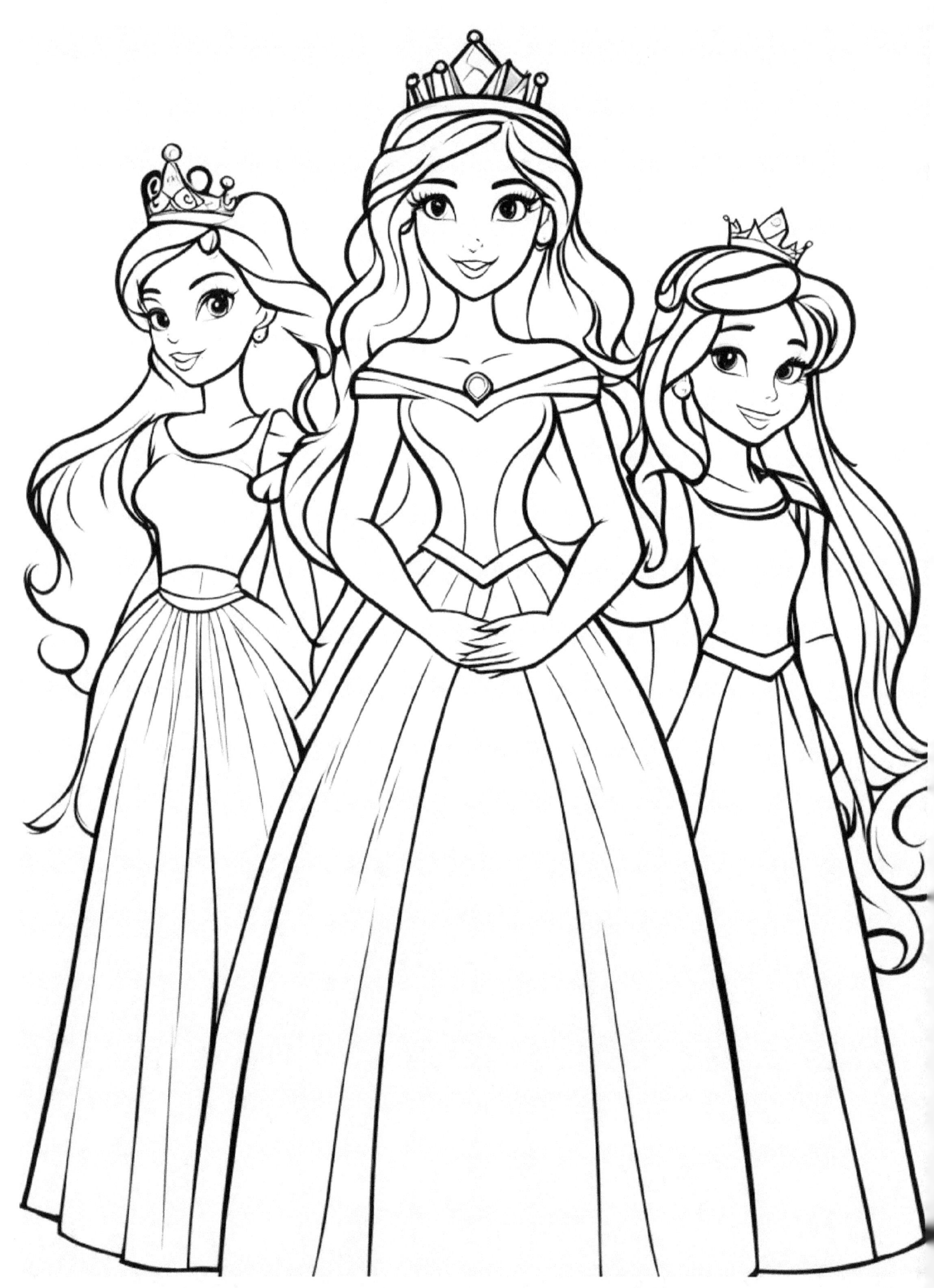

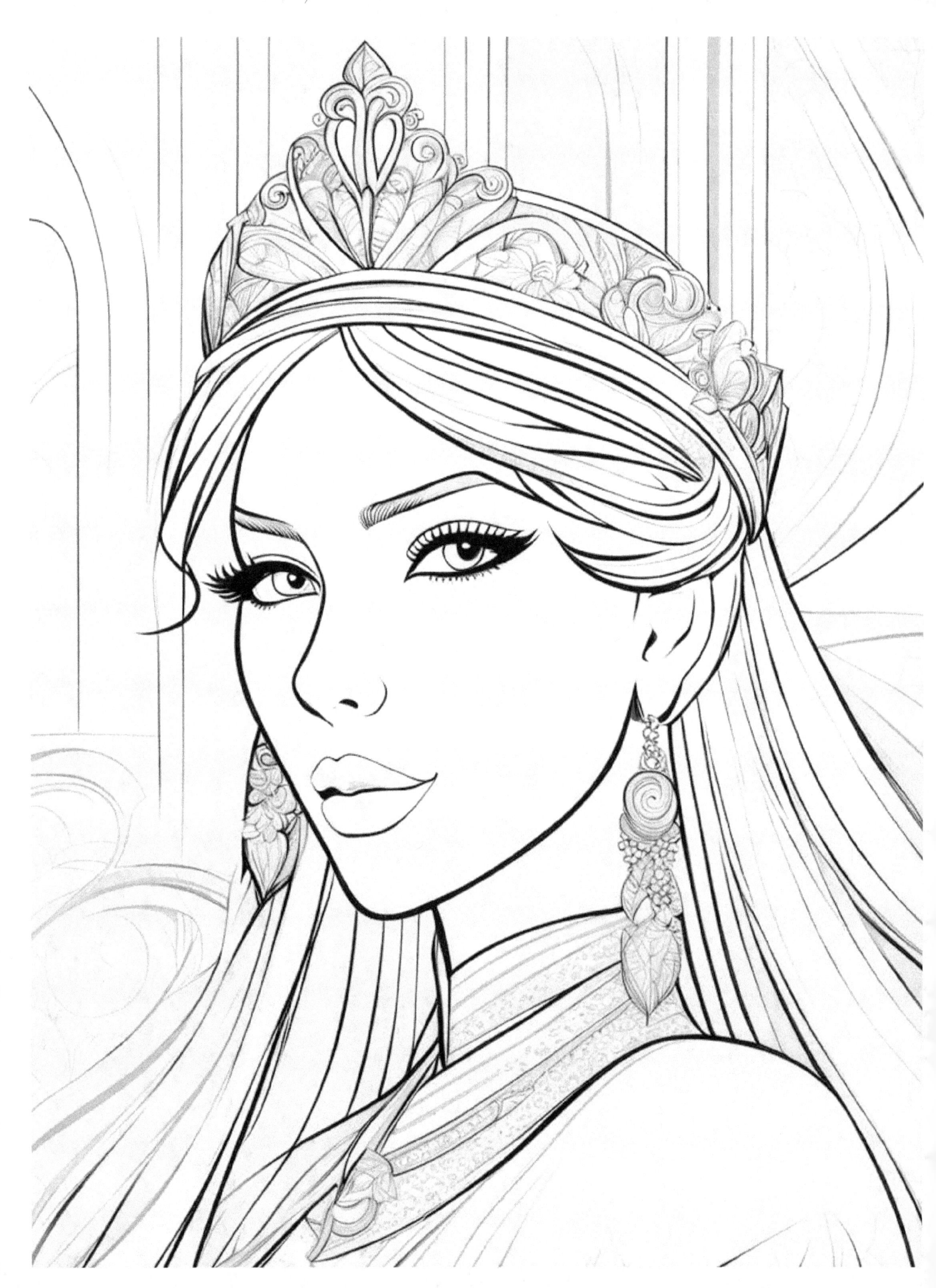

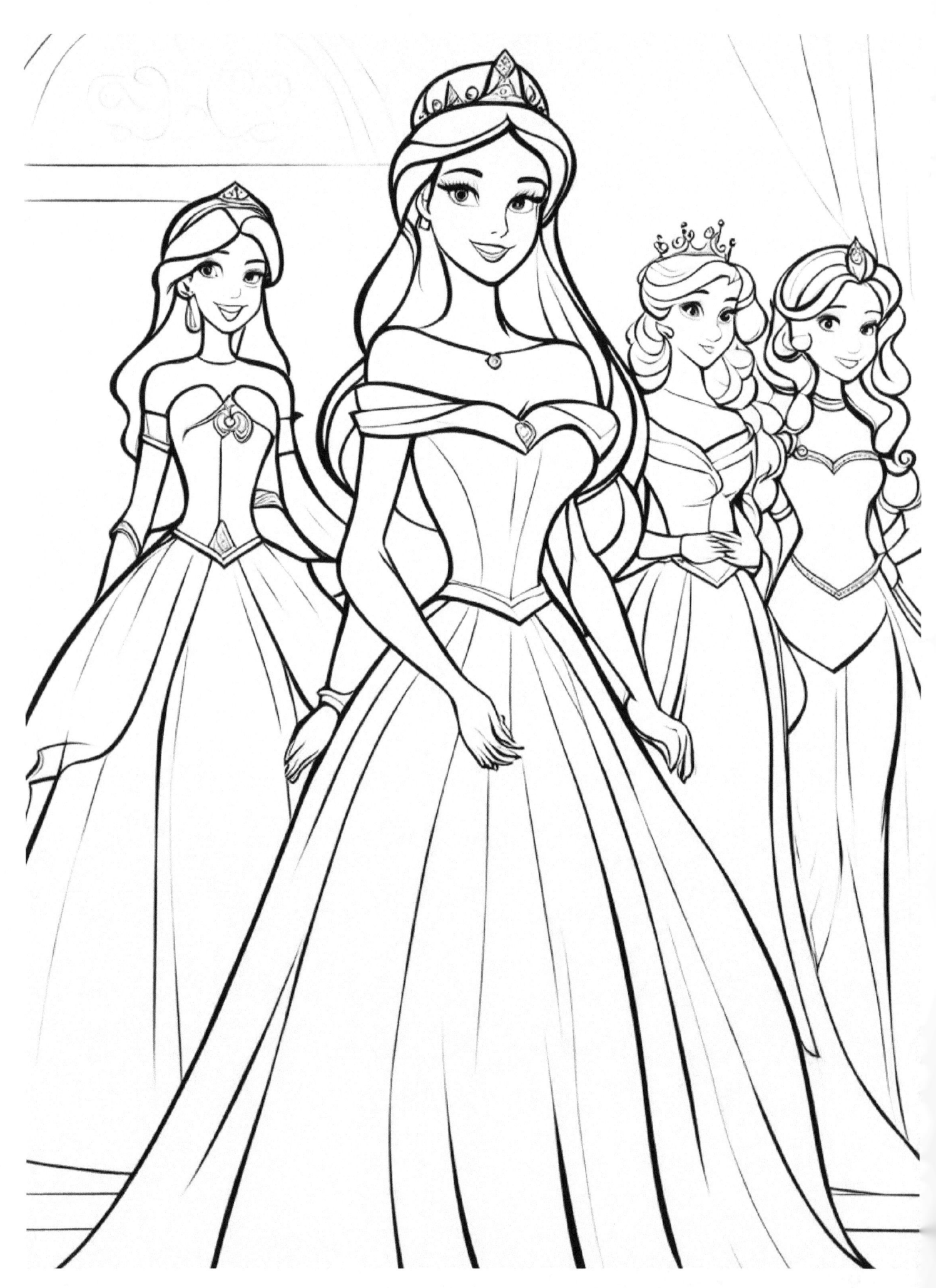

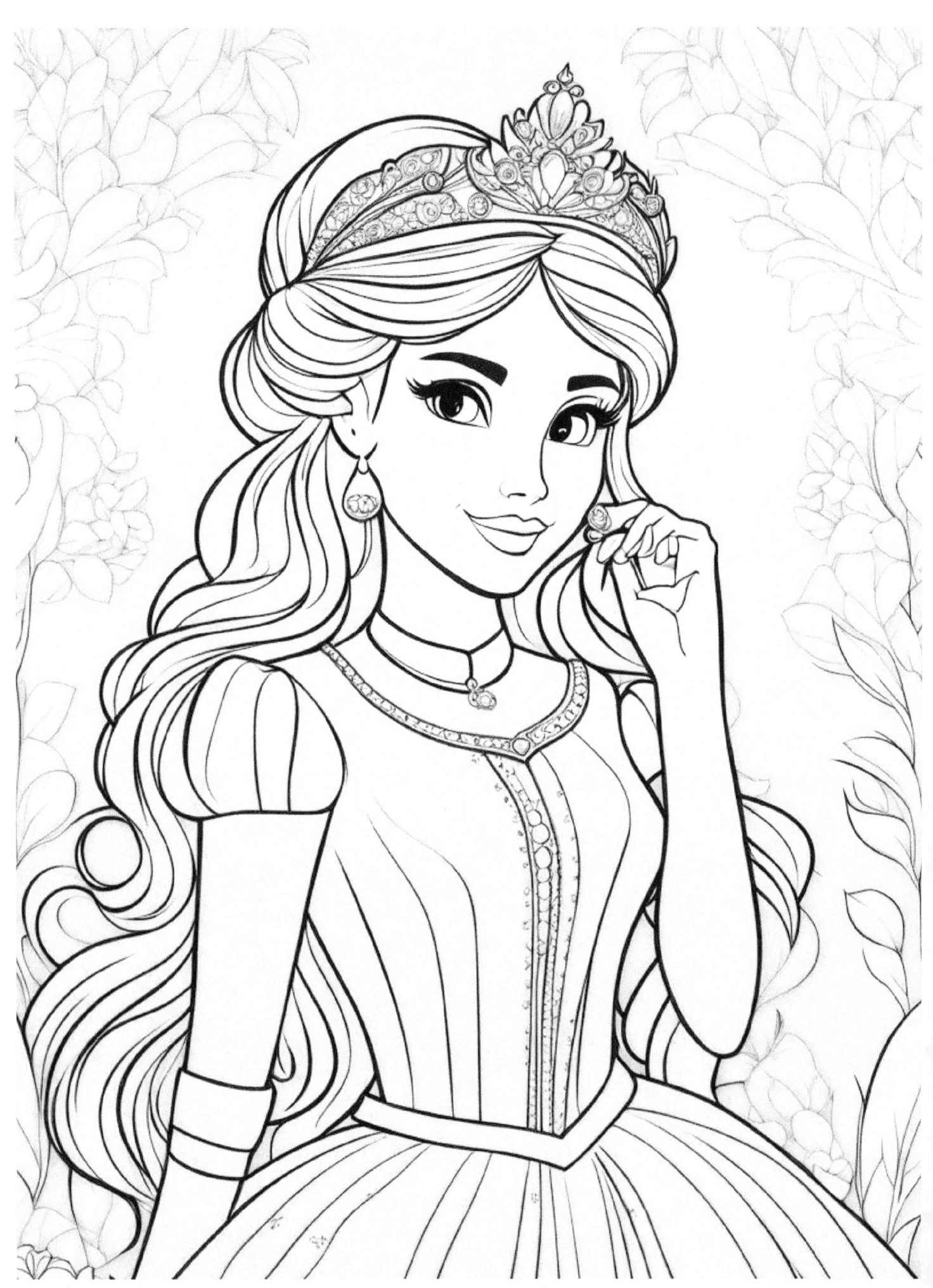

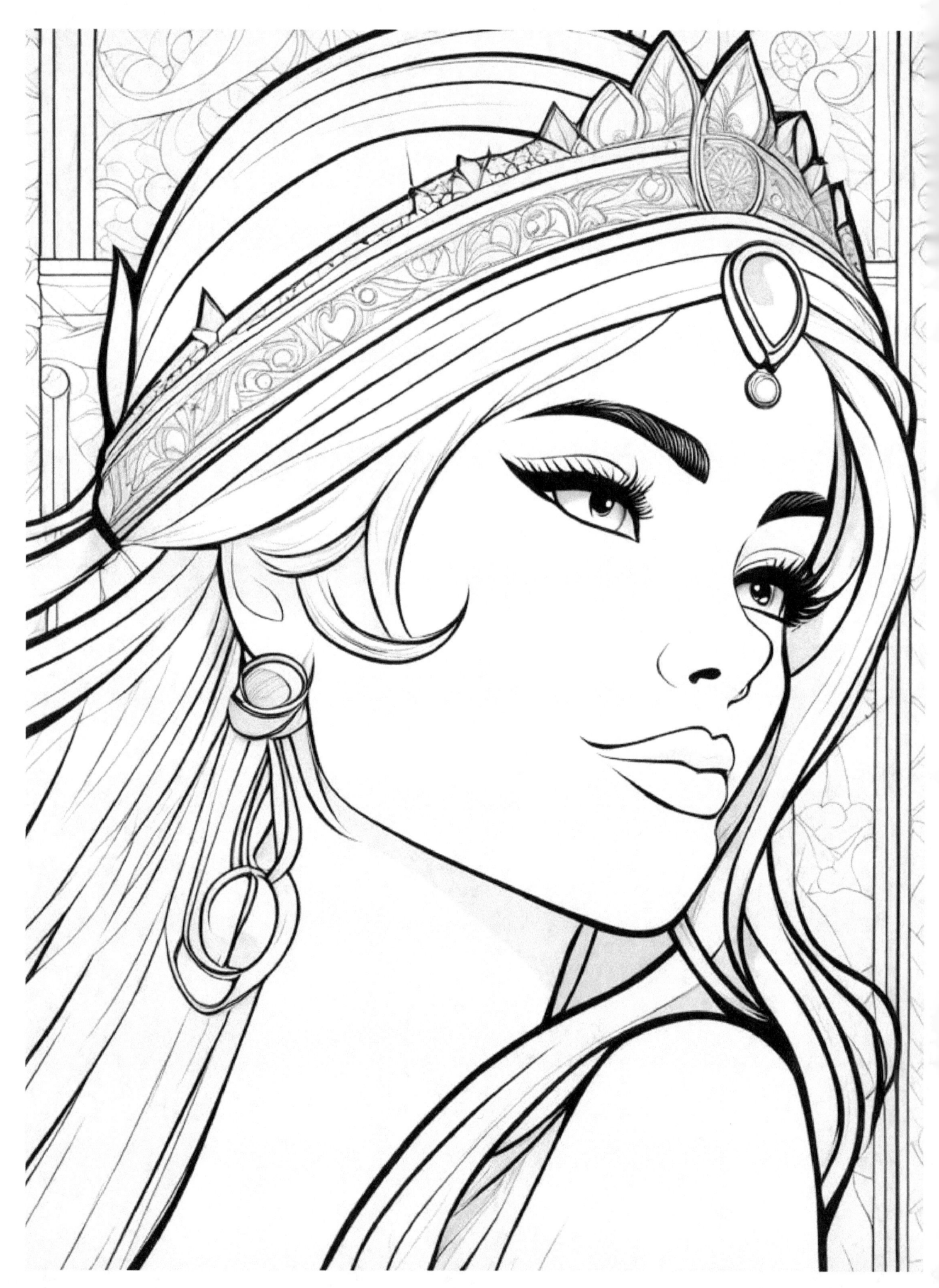

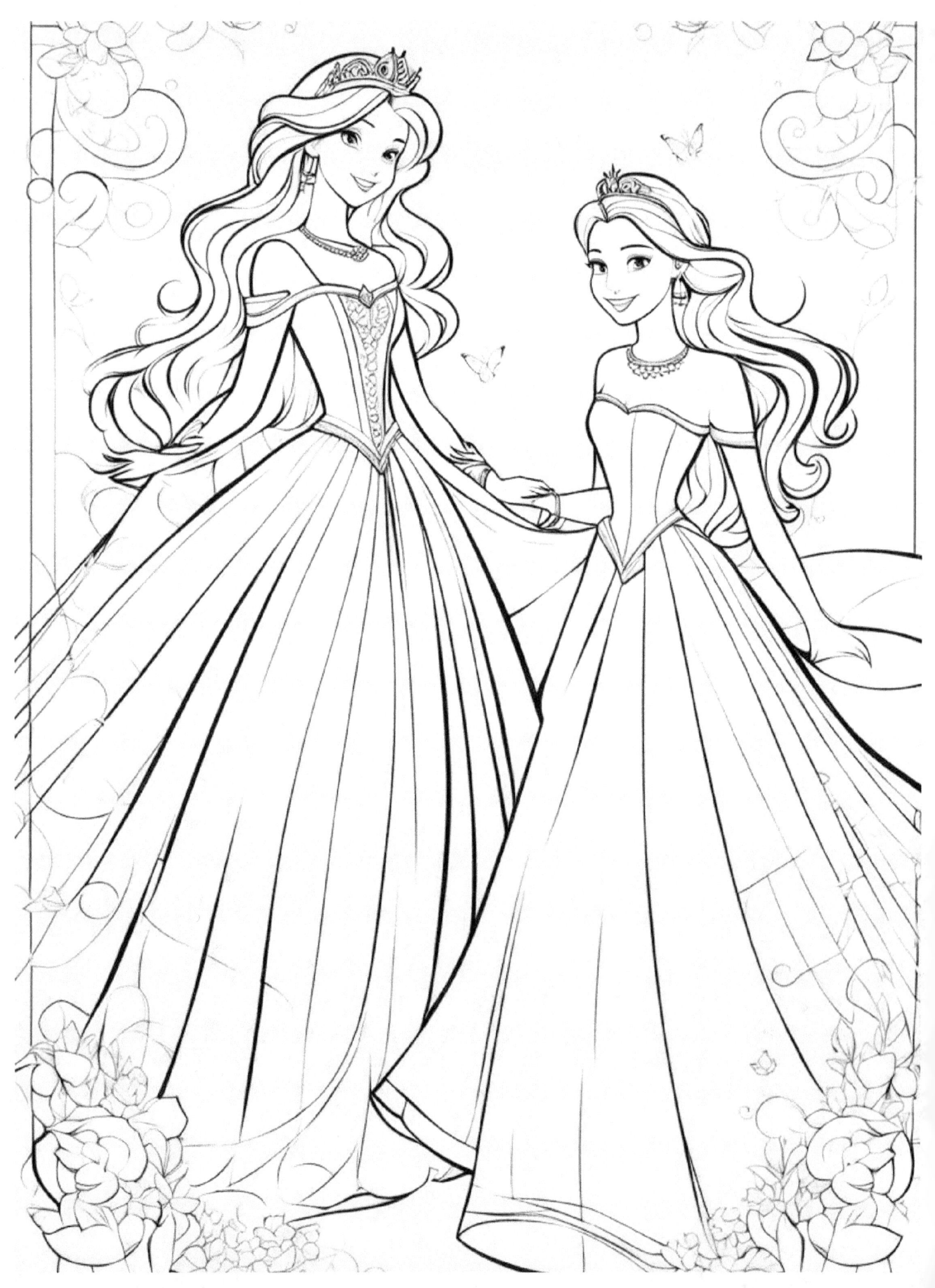

www.ingramcontent.com/pod-product-compliance
Lightning Source LLC
Chambersburg PA
CBHW062119220526
45471CB00010B/3804